Chase Hughes' Influence Code:

Mastering Persuasion in Emergency Response

Ethan Slade

"Believe you can and you're halfway there."

- Theodore Roosevelt

Disclaimer

The information and techniques presented in Chase Hughes' Influence Code: Mastering Persuasion in Emergency Response are for general educational purposes only and should not be considered as professional advice. The author and publisher disclaim any liability for any damage or injury that may result from the use of the information contained in this book. Readers are advised to consult with appropriate professionals before applying any techniques or strategies discussed in the book, especially in high-stress or emergency situations. The book's content is not intended to be a substitute for formal training or established protocols in emergency response situations. By reading this book, readers acknowledge that they understand and agree to these terms and will use the information responsibly and at their own risk. The author and publisher make no representations or warranties regarding the accuracy or completeness of the information presented, and readers should be aware that laws and regulations regarding emergency response and persuasion techniques may vary depending on their location and jurisdiction.

Copyright © 2025 Ethan Slade
All rights reserved.

Chase Hughes' Influence Code

Table of Contents

Introduction 10

Chapter 1: "Introduction to Influence in Emergency Response" 12

Understanding the Role of Influence in Emergency Response 12

The Psychology of Decision-Making in Crisis Situations 14

Building Trust and Credibility with Individuals in Distress 16

Effective Communication Strategies for Emergency Responders 18

The Impact of Emotional Intelligence on Influence in Emergency Response 21

Key Principles of Persuasion in High-Pressure Environments 23

Chapter 2: "Understanding Human Behavior in Crisis Situations" 27

Emotional Responses to Crisis 27

Psychological Factors Influencing Decision-Making 29

Group Dynamics in Emergency Situations 31

The Role of Stress and Anxiety in Human Behavior 33

Cognitive Biases and Heuristics in Crisis Environments 36

Communication Breakdowns and Conflict Escalation 39

Chapter 3: "Building Rapport and Trust with Individuals in Distress" 42

Understanding the Psychology of Distress 42

Establishing Initial Contact and Building Foundations for Rapport 44

Active Listening and Empathy in Crisis Situations 46

Cultural Sensitivity and Awareness in Building Trust 48

De-escalation Techniques for Aggressive or Resistant Individuals 50

Maintaining Boundaries and Managing Emotional Contagion 52

Chapter 4: "Effective Communication Strategies for Emergency Responders" 55

Verbal and Nonverbal Cues in Crisis Communication 55

Active Listening and Emotional Intelligence in Emergency Response .. 57

Building Rapport and Trust with Individuals in Distress 59

De-escalation Techniques for High-Pressure Situations 61

Cultural Competence and Awareness in Emergency Communication . 63

Technology-Based Communication Strategies for Emergency Responders 65

Chapter 5: "Persuasion Techniques for De-escalating Violent Encounters" 68

Establishing Rapport in High-Stress Situations 68

Active Listening Strategies for Conflict Resolution 70

Verbal De-escalation Techniques for Crisis Management 72

Nonverbal Communication Cues for Reducing Aggression 74

Managing Emotional Triggers and Empathy-Based Responses 76

Cultural Competence in De-escalating Violent Encounters 79

Chapter 6: "Influencing Group Dynamics in Emergency Response Scenarios" 82

Understanding Crowd Psychology in Emergency Situations 82

Recognizing and Managing Group Polarization 84

Strategies for De-escalating Tensions within Groups 85

The Role of Leadership in Shaping Group Dynamics 87

Communicating Effectively with Diverse Groups 89

Building Trust and Cooperation in High-Stress Environments 91

Chapter 7: "Managing Stress and Emotional Control in High-Pressure Situations" 94

Understanding the Psychological Impact of Stress on Decision-Making 94

Recognizing and Managing Emotional Triggers in High-Pressure Environments 95

Developing Resilience and Coping Strategies for Emergency Responders 97

The Role of Self-Awareness in Maintaining Emotional Control 99

Strategies for Mitigating the Effects of Chronic Stress on Performance 101

Techniques for Regulating Emotions and Staying Focused Under Pressure 103

Chapter 8: "Advanced Influence Tactics for Complex Emergency Response Situations" 105

Establishing Trust and Credibility in High-Pressure Environments 105

Leveraging Emotional Intelligence to De-Escalate Volatile Situations 107

Strategic Communication Techniques for Crisis Negotiation 109

Influence Strategies for Managing Crowd Dynamics and Behavior ... 111

Tactical Empathy and Active Listening in Emergency Response 113

Advanced Psychological Tactics for Resolving Complex Conflicts 115

Chapter 9: "Ethical Considerations and Boundaries in Emergency Response Persuasion" 119

Respecting Autonomy in High-Pressure Situations 119

Navigating Cultural and Social Biases in Persuasion 121

The Role of Deception and Misdirection in Emergency Response 123

Maintaining Professional Boundaries with Victims and Witnesses ... 126

Ethical Dilemmas in Balancing Individual Rights and Public Safety ... 129

Managing the Psychological Impact of Persuasion on Responders and Recipients 131

Chapter 10: "Mastering the Influence Code: Putting it all Together" 134

    Integrating Influence Strategies in Emergency Response 134

    Applying Emotional Intelligence in High-Pressure Situations 136

    Building Trust and Rapport with Diverse Audiences 138

    Navigating Complex Social Dynamics and Group Influences 140

    Strategic Communication Techniques for Crisis Management 143

    Sustaining Influence and Motivation in Prolonged Emergency Response Scenarios 145

Epilogue *149*

    Appendices 151

About the Author *153*

Chase Hughes' Influence Code

Introduction

The ability to persuade and influence others is a crucial skill for emergency responders, who often find themselves in high-stress situations where every decision counts. In these critical moments, the power of persuasion can be the difference between life and death. Effective communication and trust-building are essential components of this skill, enabling responders to guide individuals or crowds toward safer decisions. The National Crisis Institute has played a significant role in refining these methods, and Chase Hughes' proven techniques have been instrumental in shaping the approach outlined in this book. By mastering the art of empathic listening and strategic communication, emergency responders can defuse panic and confusion, creating a more stable environment for everyone involved. The strategies presented in this book are grounded in real-world experience, with numerous examples illustrating their application in actual crisis situations.

Emergency response scenarios are inherently unpredictable, and the ability to think on one's feet is vital. However, this does not mean that responders must rely solely on instinct or improvisation. By learning and applying Hughes' influence strategies, they can develop a systematic approach to persuasion, one that takes into account the unique dynamics of each situation. This approach recognizes that every individual or crowd is different, with distinct needs, fears, and motivations. By understanding these factors and adapting their communication style accordingly, responders can build trust and credibility, even in the most challenging circumstances. The foundation of this approach is a deep understanding of human behavior, particularly in times of crisis, and it is this foundation that will be explored in the following pages.

The influence strategies outlined in this book are not limited to emergency response situations alone, but their application in such contexts is particularly critical. By applying Hughes' methods, responders can create a safer environment for everyone involved, reducing the risk of escalation and promoting more positive outcomes. This requires a deep understanding of the complex dynamics at play in emergency situations, as well as the ability to adapt and respond effectively in high-pressure environments. The art of persuasion is not about manipulating others, but rather about building trust, establishing credibility, and communicating effectively in order to guide individuals or crowds toward safer decisions.

The following chapters will provide a detailed exploration of Hughes' Influence Code, including the core principles and strategies that underpin this approach. Through real-world examples and case studies, readers will gain a deeper understanding of how these methods can be applied in practice, and how they can be adapted to meet the unique challenges of different emergency response scenarios. By mastering the skills and techniques outlined in this book, emergency responders will be better equipped to manage volatile situations, reduce risk, and save lives. With its focus on practical application and real-world experience, 'Chase Hughes' Influence Code' is an essential resource for anyone involved in emergency response, and a valuable guide for anyone looking to develop their skills in persuasion and influence.

Chapter 1: "Introduction to Influence in Emergency Response"

Understanding the Role of Influence in Emergency Response

The role of influence in emergency response is multifaceted and critical, particularly in situations where lives are at risk. Emergency responders must be able to guide individuals or crowds toward safer decisions, often in the face of chaos and uncertainty. This requires a deep understanding of human behavior and the factors that drive decision-making in crisis situations. Research has shown that people in distress are more likely to respond to calm, authoritative, and empathetic communication, which can help to reduce panic and promote cooperation. By applying influence strategies effectively, emergency responders can create a safer environment for everyone involved, reducing the risk of escalation and promoting more positive outcomes.

Influence is not limited to verbal communication; nonverbal cues, such as body language and tone of voice, also play a significant role in shaping people's perceptions and behaviors. Emergency responders who are aware of these factors can use them to their advantage, establishing trust and credibility with individuals in distress and creating a foundation for effective communication. The National Crisis Institute's research and training programs have emphasized the importance of influence in emergency response, highlighting the need for responders to develop a range of skills, including active listening, empathy, and strategic communication.

The ability to influence others is closely tied to emotional intelligence, which enables individuals to understand and manage their own emotions, as well as those of others. Emergency responders with high emotional intelligence are better equipped to navigate complex social situations, build trust with individuals in distress, and make effective decisions under pressure. By developing their emotional intelligence and learning how to apply influence strategies effectively, emergency responders can enhance their ability to manage volatile situations and promote safer outcomes.

Effective influence in emergency response also depends on a deep understanding of the psychological and social factors that drive human behavior in crisis situations. This includes an awareness of the cognitive biases and heuristics that can influence decision-making, as well as the social and cultural norms that shape people's behaviors. By taking these factors into account, emergency responders can develop targeted strategies for influencing individuals or crowds, reducing the risk of miscommunication and promoting more positive outcomes.

The application of influence strategies in emergency response situations can have a profound impact on outcomes. For example, in hostage situations, skilled negotiators use active listening and empathy to establish trust with the perpetrator, creating an opportunity for a peaceful resolution. Similarly, in mass casualty incidents, emergency responders who can effectively communicate with panicked individuals can help to reduce chaos and promote cooperation, ultimately saving lives. The key to successful influence in these situations is a deep understanding of human behavior and the ability to adapt communication strategies to meet the needs of the individual or group.

Chase Hughes' research at the National Crisis Institute has highlighted the importance of influencing behaviors rather than simply issuing commands. This approach recognizes that people in distress are more likely to respond to suggestions and guidance that take into account their unique circumstances and concerns. By using open-ended questions, reflective listening, and non-confrontational language, emergency responders can create a collaborative environment that encourages individuals to make safe choices. This approach is particularly effective in situations where individuals may be experiencing cognitive overload or emotional distress, as it helps to reduce anxiety and promote clarity of thought.

The influence of social norms and cultural values should also be considered when developing strategies for emergency response. In some cultures, authority figures are viewed with suspicion or distrust, which can limit the effectiveness of traditional command-and-control approaches. By taking these factors into account, emergency responders can adapt their communication strategies to build trust and credibility with diverse groups, ultimately promoting safer outcomes. For instance, in communities where social cohesion is strong, emergency responders may be able to leverage existing social networks to disseminate critical information and promote cooperative behavior.

Furthermore, the use of technology, such as social media and mobile devices, can also play a crucial role in influencing behaviors during emergencies. Emergency responders can use these platforms to provide timely updates, instructions, and reassurance, helping to reduce uncertainty and promote calm. However, it is essential to consider the potential risks associated with these technologies, including the spread of misinformation and the creation of unnecessary panic. By developing strategies that take into account the complex interplay between technology, social norms, and human behavior, emergency responders can maximize the effectiveness of their influence efforts and promote safer outcomes.

Ultimately, mastering the art of influence in emergency response requires a deep understanding of human behavior, social psychology, and communication theory. By developing this expertise, emergency responders can enhance their ability to manage complex situations, reduce risk, and promote positive outcomes. The National Crisis Institute's training programs have emphasized the importance of continuous learning and skill development in this area, recognizing that effective influence is critical to saving lives and reducing harm in emergency situations.

The Psychology of Decision-Making in Crisis Situations

The Psychology of Decision-Making in Crisis Situations is a critical component of effective emergency response. When individuals are faced with life-threatening situations, their decision-making processes are significantly altered. Research has shown that people in crisis situations often experience a state of heightened emotional arousal, which can impede rational thinking and lead to impulsive decisions. This phenomenon is attributed to the activation of the brain's amygdala, a region responsible for processing emotions, particularly fear and anxiety.

In such situations, emergency responders must be equipped with the skills to influence decision-making and guide individuals toward safer choices. Chase Hughes' work at the National Crisis Institute has highlighted the importance of understanding the psychological factors that drive human behavior in crisis situations. By recognizing the role of cognitive biases, emotional influences, and social pressures, emergency responders can develop targeted strategies to mitigate risks and promote positive outcomes.

The concept of "tunnel vision" is a notable example of how crisis situations can impact decision-making. When individuals are under extreme stress, their attention narrows, and they tend to focus on a single aspect of the situation, often neglecting other critical factors. Emergency responders who are aware of this phenomenon can use strategic communication techniques to broaden the individual's perspective, encouraging them to consider alternative solutions and safer options.

Furthermore, the role of social influence in crisis decision-making cannot be overstated. In emergency situations, people often look to others for guidance and reassurance. Emergency responders who can establish trust and credibility with individuals in distress can leverage this social influence to promote cooperative behavior and reduce the risk of panic. By using empathic listening skills and non-confrontational language, responders can create a sense of calm and foster a more rational decision-making process.

The study of crisis decision-making has also revealed the significance of "mental framing" – the way in which information is presented and perceived by individuals in emergency situations. Emergency responders who can frame critical information in a clear, concise, and reassuring manner can significantly impact an individual's decision-making process, reducing confusion and anxiety while promoting safer choices. By understanding these psychological factors and developing evidence-based influence strategies, emergency responders can enhance their ability to manage crisis situations effectively and save lives.

Emergency responders must consider the psychological concept of "loss aversion" when influencing decision-making in crisis situations. Research has shown that individuals are more motivated by the fear of losing something than the prospect of gaining something. In emergency response, this means that responders can effectively use language that emphasizes the potential losses or consequences of not taking a particular action, rather than simply highlighting the benefits of compliance.

For example, in a hostage situation, a negotiator might say, "If you release the hostages now, we can work together to find a peaceful resolution and ensure your safety." This approach acknowledges the individual's concerns while also emphasizing the potential losses associated with not releasing the hostages. By framing the message in this way, the negotiator can create a sense of urgency and motivate the individual to make a safer decision.

The role of emotional intelligence in crisis decision-making is also crucial. Emergency responders who can recognize and manage their own emotions, as well as those of the individuals they are interacting with, are better equipped to de-escalate tense situations and promote positive outcomes. This involves being aware of nonverbal cues, such as body language and tone of voice, and using active listening skills to understand the individual's concerns and needs.

Chase Hughes' work at the National Crisis Institute has emphasized the importance of developing a "calm and confident" demeanor in emergency response situations. By maintaining a calm and composed attitude, responders can create a sense of stability and reassurance, which can help to reduce anxiety and promote more rational decision-making. This approach is critical in high-pressure situations, where emotions can run high and decision-making can be impaired.

The use of storytelling and narrative techniques can also be an effective way to influence decision-making in crisis situations. By sharing relevant stories or anecdotes, emergency responders can create a sense of connection and empathy with the individual, which can help to build trust and promote cooperation. For example, a responder might say, "I understand that you're scared and unsure about what to do. I've worked with people in similar situations before, and we've been able to find a safe and peaceful resolution." This approach can help to create a sense of hope and optimism, which can be a powerful motivator in crisis situations.

Ultimately, the key to effective influence in emergency response is to understand the complex psychological factors that drive human behavior in crisis situations. By recognizing the role of cognitive biases, emotional influences, and social pressures, emergency responders can develop targeted strategies to promote safer decision-making and reduce the risk of harm. By combining these insights with evidence-based communication techniques and a deep understanding of human psychology, responders can enhance their ability to manage crisis situations effectively and save lives.

Building Trust and Credibility with Individuals in Distress

Building trust and credibility with individuals in distress is a critical component of effective emergency response. When people are faced with life-threatening situations, their ability to think clearly and make rational decisions is often impaired. In these moments, the role of the emergency responder is not only to provide assistance but also to guide the individual toward safer choices. This requires a deep understanding of human psychology and behavior, as well as the ability to establish trust and credibility in a matter of seconds.

Research has shown that individuals in crisis situations are more likely to follow instructions and comply with requests when they perceive the emergency responder as trustworthy and credible. This is because trust and credibility are closely tied to feelings of safety and security. When individuals feel safe, they are more likely to be receptive to guidance and direction. Chase Hughes' work at the National Crisis Institute has highlighted the importance of establishing a rapport with individuals in distress, using techniques such as active listening and empathic understanding.

Active listening involves fully engaging with the individual, paying attention to their words, tone, and body language. This helps to create a sense of connection and understanding, which is essential for building trust. Empathic understanding takes this a step further, by acknowledging the individual's emotions and validating their experience. For example, an emergency responder might say, "I can see that you're scared and upset. I'm here to help you, and I'll do everything I can to keep you safe." This approach helps to create a sense of calm and reassurance, which can be a powerful antidote to panic and confusion.

The use of non-verbal communication is also critical in building trust and credibility with individuals in distress. Emergency responders who maintain eye contact, use open and approachable body language, and speak in a calm and clear tone are more likely to be perceived as trustworthy and credible. Conversely, responders who appear aggressive, dismissive, or uncaring are likely to exacerbate the situation, leading to increased anxiety and resistance.

In high-pressure situations, every second counts. Emergency responders must be able to establish trust and credibility quickly, often in a matter of seconds. This requires a deep understanding of human psychology and behavior, as well as the ability to remain calm and composed under pressure. By combining these skills with evidence-based communication techniques, emergency responders can build trust and credibility with individuals in distress, guiding them toward safer decisions and reducing the risk of harm.

Establishing trust and credibility with individuals in distress requires a nuanced understanding of their emotional state. When people are under stress, their ability to process information is impaired, and they become more susceptible to emotional influences. Emergency responders must be aware of these dynamics and adapt their communication approach accordingly. Chase Hughes' influence code emphasizes the importance of empathy and validation in building trust with individuals in crisis situations.

For instance, in a hostage situation, an emergency responder might use empathic language to acknowledge the individual's feelings and concerns. This could involve statements like, "I understand that you're feeling desperate and scared, and I'm here to help you find a way out of this situation." By acknowledging the individual's emotions, the responder creates a sense of connection and understanding, which can help to reduce tension and increase cooperation.

The use of mirroring techniques can also be an effective way to build trust and credibility with individuals in distress. Mirroring involves reflecting the individual's body language, tone, and language to create a sense of rapport and connection. For example, if an individual is speaking in a calm and measured tone, the emergency responder should respond in a similar manner. This helps to create a sense of mutual understanding and can increase the individual's willingness to follow instructions.

In addition to verbal communication, non-verbal cues play a critical role in building trust and credibility with individuals in distress. Emergency responders must be aware of their body language and ensure that it is open, approachable, and non-threatening. This could involve maintaining eye contact, using open and relaxed posture, and avoiding aggressive or confrontational gestures.

The influence code also emphasizes the importance of transparency and honesty in building trust with individuals in crisis situations. Emergency responders must be clear and direct in their communication, avoiding ambiguity or mixed messages. This helps to create a sense of trust and credibility, as individuals are more likely to cooperate with someone who is transparent and honest about their intentions.

In high-pressure situations, emergency responders must be able to think on their feet and adapt their communication approach to the individual's needs. This requires a deep understanding of human psychology and behavior, as well as the ability to remain calm and composed under pressure. By combining these skills with evidence-based communication techniques, emergency responders can build trust and credibility with individuals in distress, guiding them toward safer decisions and reducing the risk of harm.

Chase Hughes' work has demonstrated that building trust and credibility with individuals in distress is a critical component of effective crisis management. By establishing a rapport with the individual, using empathic language, and adapting to their emotional state, emergency responders can increase cooperation and reduce the risk of escalation. As the influence code continues to evolve, it is likely to play an increasingly important role in shaping the way emergency responders interact with individuals in crisis situations, ultimately saving lives and reducing harm.

Effective Communication Strategies for Emergency Responders

Effective communication is the foundation of successful emergency response. In high-pressure situations, clear and strategic communication can mean the difference between life and death. Chase Hughes' influence code emphasizes the importance of building trust and establishing a rapport with individuals in distress. This requires a deep understanding of human psychology and behavior, as well as the ability to adapt communication approaches to the individual's needs.

Emergency responders must be able to communicate effectively in a variety of contexts, from crowd control to one-on-one interactions with hostages or victims. In each situation, the goal is to guide individuals toward safer decisions, reducing the risk of harm and promoting a peaceful resolution. Hughes' methods, refined at the National Crisis Institute, provide a proven framework for achieving this goal.

A critical component of effective communication in emergency response is empathic listening. This involves actively engaging with the individual, paying attention to their words, tone, and body language. By acknowledging and validating the individual's emotions, emergency responders can create a sense of connection and understanding, which is essential for building trust. For example, in a hostage situation, an emergency responder might use empathic listening to establish a rapport with the hostage-taker, creating an opportunity for negotiation and de-escalation.

Strategic communication is also critical in emergency response situations. This involves using clear and concise language, avoiding ambiguity or mixed messages, and adapting communication approaches to the individual's needs. Emergency responders must be able to think on their feet, responding quickly and effectively to changing situations. By combining empathic listening with strategic communication, emergency responders can defuse panic and confusion, promoting a safer and more peaceful outcome.

Real-world examples demonstrate the effectiveness of Hughes' influence strategies in emergency response situations. For instance, during a riot, emergency responders used empathic listening and strategic communication to establish a rapport with crowd leaders, ultimately de-escalating the situation and preventing further violence. In another example, an emergency responder used Hughes' methods to negotiate with a hostage-taker, securing the safe release of the hostages and avoiding a tragic outcome.

By mastering the art of trust-building, empathic listening, and strategic communication, emergency responders can save lives and reduce harm in critical moments. The influence code provides a comprehensive framework for achieving this goal, offering a powerful tool for anyone managing volatile situations. In the following sections, we will explore the key components of effective communication strategies for emergency responders, providing a detailed analysis of Hughes' methods and their application in real-world scenarios.

Effective communication strategies for emergency responders require a deep understanding of human behavior and psychology. Hughes' influence code provides a framework for emergency responders to build trust, establish rapport, and guide individuals toward safer decisions. A key component of this framework is the use of mirroring techniques, which involve reflecting an individual's body language, tone, and language to create a sense of connection and understanding.

Mirroring can be particularly effective in high-stress situations, such as hostage negotiations or crowd control. By mirroring the individual's behavior, emergency responders can create a sense of calm and reduce tension, making it easier to communicate and find a peaceful resolution. For example, during a hostage situation, an emergency responder might mirror the hostage-taker's tone and language to establish a rapport and build trust.

Another critical aspect of effective communication in emergency response is active listening. This involves paying close attention to the individual's words, tone, and body language, and responding in a way that acknowledges and validates their emotions. Active listening can help emergency responders to identify underlying concerns or motivations, and address them in a way that promotes a peaceful resolution.

Hughes' influence code also emphasizes the importance of using open-ended questions in emergency response situations. Open-ended questions encourage individuals to share more information and provide insight into their thoughts and feelings, making it easier for emergency responders to understand their needs and concerns. For example, during a crowd control situation, an emergency responder might use open-ended questions to engage with crowd leaders and understand their motivations, ultimately finding a way to de-escalate the situation.

The influence code provides a range of strategies and techniques for emergency responders to communicate effectively in high-pressure situations. These include using positive language, avoiding confrontational tone, and focusing on solutions rather than problems. By mastering these techniques, emergency responders can build trust, establish rapport, and guide individuals toward safer decisions, ultimately saving lives and reducing harm.

Real-world examples demonstrate the effectiveness of Hughes' influence strategies in emergency response situations. For instance, during a mass casualty incident, emergency responders used mirroring and active listening to calm and reassure victims, ultimately reducing stress and promoting a more efficient evacuation process. In another example, an emergency responder used open-ended questions to engage with a crowd leader, understanding their motivations and finding a way to de-escalate the situation without resorting to force.

By providing a comprehensive framework for effective communication in emergency response situations, Hughes' influence code offers a powerful tool for emergency responders to save lives and reduce harm. The strategies and techniques outlined in the influence code can be applied in a range of contexts, from crowd control to one-on-one interactions with hostages or victims. By mastering these skills, emergency responders can become more effective communicators, ultimately promoting safer and more peaceful outcomes in critical moments.

The Impact of Emotional Intelligence on Influence in Emergency Response

The Impact of Emotional Intelligence on Influence in Emergency Response

Emotional intelligence plays a crucial role in effective influence during emergency response situations. Chase Hughes' influence code emphasizes the importance of understanding and managing emotions to guide individuals toward safer decisions. In high-pressure situations, emotional intelligence enables emergency responders to remain calm, think critically, and communicate effectively.

Emergency responders with high emotional intelligence can better understand the emotional states of those they interact with, whether it's a crowd, a hostage, or a victim. This understanding allows them to tailor their communication approach to the individual's emotional needs, building trust and rapport in the process. For instance, during a riot, an emergency responder with high emotional intelligence might recognize the emotional contagion effect, where the emotions of one person can spread quickly to others. By acknowledging and addressing these emotions, the responder can create a sense of calm and reduce the likelihood of further escalation.

Hughes' influence code highlights the significance of self-awareness in emotional intelligence. Emergency responders must be able to recognize and manage their own emotions to maintain a clear and level head in critical situations. This self-awareness enables them to make rational decisions, rather than reacting impulsively to emotional stimuli. In a hostage situation, for example, an emergency responder with high self-awareness might recognize the emotional toll of the situation on themselves and take steps to manage their own stress, ensuring they remain focused and effective in their communication with the hostage-taker.

The ability to empathize with others is another critical aspect of emotional intelligence in emergency response. By putting themselves in the shoes of those they interact with, emergency responders can better understand their needs, concerns, and motivations. This empathy enables them to communicate more effectively, using language and tone that resonates with the individual or crowd. In a mass evacuation scenario, for instance, an emergency responder with high empathy might recognize the fear and anxiety of those being evacuated, providing reassurance and clear instructions to reduce panic and promote a safe and orderly exit.

Real-world examples demonstrate the effectiveness of emotional intelligence in emergency response situations. During a recent natural disaster, emergency responders used emotional intelligence to calm and reassure victims, providing critical support and guidance during a traumatic event. By understanding and managing emotions, these responders were able to build trust and facilitate a more efficient evacuation process, ultimately saving lives.

By incorporating emotional intelligence into their influence strategies, emergency responders can become more effective communicators, better equipped to handle the complex emotional dynamics of critical situations. Hughes' influence code provides a comprehensive framework for developing emotional intelligence in emergency response, empowering responders to make a positive impact in high-pressure situations.

Emotional intelligence is not only crucial for emergency responders, but also for the individuals they interact with during critical situations. When responders demonstrate high emotional intelligence, they create a positive emotional contagion effect, where their calm and composed demeanor helps to reduce stress and anxiety in those around them. This, in turn, facilitates more effective communication and cooperation.

Hughes' influence code emphasizes the importance of recognizing and managing emotional triggers in emergency response situations. Emotional triggers can escalate tensions and lead to impulsive decisions, which can have devastating consequences. By understanding and addressing these triggers, emergency responders can create a safer and more controlled environment. For example, during a hostage situation, an emergency responder might recognize that the hostage-taker is emotionally triggered by a particular topic or phrase. By avoiding this trigger and using empathetic language, the responder can reduce the likelihood of escalation and increase the chances of a peaceful resolution.

The role of emotional intelligence in building trust is also critical in emergency response situations. When emergency responders demonstrate empathy, active listening, and a genuine interest in the well-being of those they interact with, they build trust and establish a positive relationship. This trust enables individuals to feel more comfortable sharing information, following instructions, and cooperating with responders. In a mass casualty incident, for instance, emergency responders with high emotional intelligence might use empathetic communication to reassure victims and their families, providing critical support and guidance during a traumatic event.

Chase Hughes' influence code provides a structured approach to developing emotional intelligence in emergency response situations. The code emphasizes the importance of self-awareness, empathy, and social skills, providing responders with the tools they need to navigate complex emotional dynamics. By incorporating this code into their training and operations, emergency response organizations can improve the effectiveness of their responders, reduce the risk of escalation, and ultimately save lives.

Real-world applications of Hughes' influence code demonstrate its effectiveness in emergency response situations. During a recent active shooter incident, emergency responders used the code to de-escalate tensions and establish communication with the shooter. By recognizing and addressing emotional triggers, the responders were able to create a safe and controlled environment, ultimately resolving the situation without further violence. This example highlights the critical role of emotional intelligence in emergency response and the importance of incorporating Hughes' influence code into responder training and operations.

By developing emotional intelligence and applying Hughes' influence code, emergency responders can become more effective communicators, better equipped to handle the complex emotional dynamics of critical situations. This, in turn, enables them to build trust, reduce tensions, and ultimately save lives. As the field of emergency response continues to evolve, the importance of emotional intelligence and influence strategies will only continue to grow, making it essential for responders to prioritize these skills in their training and operations.

Key Principles of Persuasion in High-Pressure Environments

Key Principles of Persuasion in High-Pressure Environments

Persuasion is a critical component of emergency response, enabling responders to guide individuals or crowds toward safer decisions in high-pressure situations. Chase Hughes' influence code provides a comprehensive framework for mastering persuasion in emergency response, drawing on his expertise and experience at the National Crisis Institute. The code is built around key principles that empower responders to build trust, listen empathetically, and communicate strategically, defusing panic and confusion in the process.

Effective persuasion in high-pressure environments requires a deep understanding of human behavior and psychology. Emergency responders must be able to read people quickly, recognizing emotional cues, motivations, and concerns. This enables them to tailor their approach to the individual or crowd, using language and tone that resonates with their audience. For example, during a riot, a responder might recognize that the crowd is driven by anger and frustration, using empathetic language to acknowledge these emotions and redirect the crowd's energy toward a more constructive outlet.

Trust-building is a fundamental principle of persuasion in high-pressure environments. When individuals or crowds trust emergency responders, they are more likely to follow instructions, share information, and cooperate with response efforts. Responders can build trust by demonstrating empathy, active listening, and a genuine interest in the well-being of those they interact with. In a hostage standoff, for instance, a responder might establish a rapport with the hostage-taker, using open and honest communication to build trust and create a sense of mutual understanding.

Strategic communication is another critical principle of persuasion in high-pressure environments. Emergency responders must be able to communicate clearly and concisely, conveying complex information in a way that is easy to understand. This requires a deep understanding of the audience, including their concerns, motivations, and level of knowledge. For example, during a mass evacuation, a responder might use simple, direct language to inform people of the evacuation route and any necessary safety precautions, minimizing confusion and panic in the process.

Chase Hughes' influence code provides a structured approach to applying these principles in high-pressure environments. The code emphasizes the importance of flexibility and adaptability, enabling responders to adjust their approach as situations evolve and unfold. By mastering the key principles of persuasion, emergency responders can become more effective communicators, better equipped to manage volatile situations and save lives. Real-world examples demonstrate the effectiveness of Hughes' influence strategies, from de-escalating violent confrontations to coordinating complex rescue operations.

The influence code is grounded in a deep understanding of human psychology and behavior, recognizing that people are driven by emotions, motivations, and concerns. By acknowledging and addressing these factors, emergency responders can build trust, establish rapport, and guide individuals or crowds toward safer decisions. The code's emphasis on empathy, active listening, and strategic communication provides a powerful framework for persuasion in high-pressure environments, enabling responders to navigate complex situations with confidence and precision.

Chase Hughes' Influence Code: Mastering Persuasion in Emergency Response

The influence code's emphasis on empathy and active listening enables emergency responders to establish a deep understanding of the individuals or crowds they interact with. This understanding is critical in high-pressure environments, where emotions run high and decisions must be made quickly. By acknowledging and addressing the emotional needs of those involved, responders can create a sense of safety and trust, reducing the likelihood of escalation and increasing the chances of a peaceful resolution.

A key aspect of empathy in emergency response is recognizing the role of emotional triggers. Emotional triggers are stimuli that can escalate tensions and lead to impulsive decisions, such as a particular phrase or topic that triggers anger or aggression. By identifying and avoiding these triggers, responders can create a more stable environment, reducing the risk of violence and promoting a more constructive dialogue. For example, during a hostage negotiation, a responder might recognize that the hostage-taker is triggered by references to their past mistakes, using this knowledge to tailor their communication approach and avoid escalating the situation.

Strategic communication is also critical in high-pressure environments, where clear and concise messaging can mean the difference between life and death. Emergency responders must be able to convey complex information quickly and effectively, using language that is easy to understand and free from ambiguity. This requires a deep understanding of the audience, including their level of knowledge, concerns, and motivations. For instance, during a natural disaster response, a responder might use simple, direct language to inform people of evacuation routes and safety precautions, minimizing confusion and panic in the process.

Chase Hughes' influence code provides a range of tools and techniques for applying these principles in high-pressure environments. The code includes strategies for building trust, establishing rapport, and communicating effectively, as well as tactics for managing conflict and de-escalating violent situations. By mastering these skills, emergency responders can become more effective communicators, better equipped to manage complex situations and save lives.

Real-world examples demonstrate the effectiveness of Hughes' influence strategies in a range of high-pressure environments. For example, during a recent riot response, emergency responders used empathy and active listening to establish a rapport with crowd leaders, reducing tensions and promoting a peaceful resolution. In another instance, a hostage negotiator used strategic communication to establish a dialogue with a hostage-taker, ultimately securing the safe release of the hostages.

The influence code's emphasis on flexibility and adaptability is also critical in high-pressure environments, where situations can evolve rapidly and unpredictably. By remaining flexible and adaptable, emergency responders can adjust their approach as needed, responding to changing circumstances and staying focused on their goals. This requires a deep understanding of the situation, including the individuals involved, the environment, and the available resources.

Ultimately, Chase Hughes' influence code provides a powerful framework for persuasion in high-pressure environments, enabling emergency responders to build trust, establish rapport, and communicate effectively. By mastering the key principles of empathy, active listening, and strategic communication, responders can become more effective communicators, better equipped to manage complex situations and save lives. The code's emphasis on flexibility, adaptability, and real-world application makes it an essential tool for anyone working in emergency response, from law enforcement and firefighting to disaster relief and crisis management.

Chapter 2: "Understanding Human Behavior in Crisis Situations"

Emotional Responses to Crisis

Emotional responses to crisis situations are complex and multifaceted, driven by a combination of psychological, neurological, and environmental factors. In high-pressure environments, individuals often experience a surge in stress hormones such as adrenaline and cortisol, which can impair cognitive function and lead to impulsive decision-making. This phenomenon is evident in emergency response scenarios, where panicked individuals may engage in risky behaviors, such as fleeing from danger without regard for their safety or the safety of others.

Research has shown that emotional arousal can significantly impact an individual's ability to process information and make rational decisions. When people are under extreme stress, their brains tend to rely on mental shortcuts, known as heuristics, which can lead to biased thinking and poor judgment. For instance, in a crisis situation, an individual may overestimate the severity of the threat or underestimate their ability to cope with it, resulting in excessive fear or anxiety.

Emergency responders must be aware of these emotional dynamics and develop strategies to mitigate their negative effects. By acknowledging and addressing the emotional needs of individuals in crisis, responders can create a sense of calm and stability, reducing the likelihood of panic and promoting more constructive behaviors. This requires a deep understanding of human psychology and behavior, as well as effective communication skills, empathy, and active listening.

The National Crisis Institute's research has identified several key factors that influence emotional responses to crisis situations, including perceived control, social support, and prior experience with traumatic events. Individuals who feel a sense of control over their environment or have access to strong social support networks tend to exhibit more resilient behaviors in the face of adversity. Conversely, those who have experienced trauma in the past may be more prone to emotional distress and impulsive decision-making.

By understanding these factors and developing targeted interventions, emergency responders can better manage the emotional responses of individuals in crisis, reducing the risk of harm and promoting safer outcomes. Chase Hughes' influence code provides a comprehensive framework for addressing these challenges, offering evidence-based strategies for building trust, establishing rapport, and communicating effectively in high-pressure environments.

Emergency responders must consider the role of emotional contagion in crisis situations, where the emotions of one individual can rapidly spread to others. This phenomenon can create a ripple effect, amplifying fear, anxiety, or panic within a group. For example, during a mass evacuation, an individual's frantic behavior can infect others, leading to a surge in chaotic and potentially dangerous actions. By recognizing the potential for emotional contagion, responders can develop strategies to mitigate its impact, such as identifying and calming key influencers within the group.

The influence of group dynamics on emotional responses to crisis situations is also critical. When individuals are part of a cohesive group, they tend to exhibit more resilient behaviors and better decision-making. In contrast, fragmented or anonymous groups often experience increased fear, mistrust, and chaotic behavior. Emergency responders can leverage this knowledge by establishing clear lines of communication, promoting social bonding, and fostering a sense of community among those affected by the crisis.

Chase Hughes' influence code emphasizes the importance of empathy and active listening in managing emotional responses to crisis situations. By acknowledging and validating individuals' emotions, responders can establish trust and create a safe environment for open communication. This approach enables responders to gather critical information, address concerns, and provide targeted support, ultimately reducing the risk of further escalation.

Effective communication is also crucial in shaping emotional responses to crisis situations. Responders must be aware of the potential for misinterpretation or misinformation, which can exacerbate fear and anxiety. Clear, concise, and transparent communication can help alleviate uncertainty, reduce rumors, and promote a sense of control among those affected. The National Crisis Institute's research highlights the value of using simple, straightforward language, avoiding jargon, and providing regular updates to maintain trust and credibility.

In addition to these strategies, emergency responders must be aware of their own emotional responses to crisis situations. The stress and trauma associated with responding to emergencies can take a toll on responders' mental health, impairing their ability to make sound decisions and provide effective support. By prioritizing self-care, recognizing the signs of burnout, and seeking support when needed, responders can maintain their emotional resilience and provide optimal care to those in need.

By understanding the complex interplay of factors influencing emotional responses to crisis situations, emergency responders can develop targeted interventions to mitigate the negative effects of stress, fear, and anxiety. Chase Hughes' influence code offers a comprehensive framework for addressing these challenges, providing responders with the tools and strategies necessary to promote safer outcomes, reduce harm, and support those affected by crisis situations.

Psychological Factors Influencing Decision-Making

Psychological factors play a crucial role in shaping decision-making processes during crisis situations. Emergency responders must consider the cognitive biases, emotional influences, and social pressures that affect individuals' choices under stress. Research conducted at the National Crisis Institute highlights the significance of understanding these psychological factors, as they can either hinder or facilitate effective decision-making.

In high-pressure environments, individuals often rely on mental shortcuts, known as heuristics, to make rapid decisions. These cognitive biases can lead to systematic errors in judgment, such as overestimating the severity of a threat or underestimating the effectiveness of a response strategy. For example, during a mass evacuation, people may prioritize following the crowd rather than seeking alternative escape routes, due to the influence of social proof heuristic.

Emotional states also significantly impact decision-making processes in crisis situations. Fear, anxiety, and stress can impede cognitive function, leading to impulsive choices that may compromise safety. The National Crisis Institute's research demonstrates that emotional arousal can reduce an individual's ability to process information, making them more susceptible to misinformation and manipulation. Effective emergency responders must be able to recognize and address these emotional influences, using strategies such as empathic listening and trust-building to calm affected individuals and promote more rational decision-making.

The role of social influence in shaping decision-making processes cannot be overstated. In crisis situations, individuals often look to others for guidance and reassurance, making them more likely to follow the actions of those around them. This phenomenon can lead to a cascade effect, where a single individual's decision influences the choices of others, potentially resulting in a collective response that is either beneficial or detrimental. Emergency responders must be aware of these social dynamics and use targeted communication strategies to promote positive behaviors and mitigate the spread of misinformation.

Chase Hughes' influence code provides a comprehensive framework for understanding and addressing the psychological factors that influence decision-making in crisis situations. By recognizing the interplay between cognitive biases, emotional states, and social pressures, emergency responders can develop effective strategies to guide individuals toward safer choices. The following sections will explore these concepts in greater depth, providing evidence-based insights and real-world examples to illustrate the application of Hughes' influence code in critical moments.

Emergency responders must consider the impact of psychological anchors on decision-making processes in crisis situations. Anchoring occurs when individuals rely too heavily on the first piece of information they receive, using it as a reference point for subsequent decisions. For example, during a hostage situation, if the initial report indicates that the perpetrator is armed with a high-powered rifle, responders may overestimate the threat level and adjust their tactics accordingly, even if later information suggests that the weapon is actually a handgun.

The availability heuristic also plays a significant role in decision-making under stress. This cognitive bias leads individuals to overestimate the importance of vivid or memorable events, simply because they are more easily recalled. In a crisis situation, responders may prioritize mitigating the most dramatic or attention-grabbing hazards, rather than addressing the most likely or probable threats. The National Crisis Institute's research highlights the need for emergency responders to be aware of this bias and to seek out diverse sources of information to ensure a more comprehensive understanding of the situation.

Emotional contagion is another critical psychological factor that influences decision-making in crisis situations. When individuals are exposed to the emotions of those around them, they can "catch" and mirror those feelings, leading to a collective emotional state that may impede or facilitate effective decision-making. For instance, during a natural disaster, if emergency responders convey a sense of calm and confidence, affected individuals are more likely to remain calm and follow instructions, whereas panic and anxiety can spread rapidly if responders appear flustered or uncertain.

Chase Hughes' influence code provides strategies for mitigating the negative effects of these psychological factors on decision-making. By recognizing the potential for cognitive biases, emotional influences, and social pressures, emergency responders can develop targeted communication techniques to promote more rational and informed choices. For example, using clear and concise language, avoiding emotive appeals, and providing multiple sources of information can help to reduce the impact of anchoring and availability heuristics. Additionally, responders can use emotional regulation techniques, such as deep breathing and active listening, to manage their own emotions and create a more stable environment for decision-making.

The effective application of Hughes' influence code requires a deep understanding of the psychological factors that shape human behavior in crisis situations. By considering the complex interplay between cognitive biases, emotional states, and social pressures, emergency responders can develop evidence-based strategies to guide individuals toward safer choices and promote more effective decision-making under stress.

Group Dynamics in Emergency Situations

Group dynamics play a crucial role in shaping the behavior of individuals in emergency situations. During critical moments, such as riots or mass evacuations, the actions of those around them can significantly influence an individual's decisions and reactions. Chase Hughes' research at the National Crisis Institute has identified key factors that contribute to the formation of group dynamics in emergency situations, including social identity, norms, and emotional contagion.

Social identity theory suggests that individuals derive a sense of belonging and identity from the groups they belong to. In emergency situations, this can lead to a strong desire to conform to the actions and behaviors of others within the group. For example, during a riot, individuals may engage in destructive behavior simply because others around them are doing so, rather than due to any personal motivation or grievance. Emergency responders must be aware of these social identity dynamics and use targeted communication strategies to promote a sense of shared identity and purpose that aligns with safe and constructive behaviors.

Group norms also exert a powerful influence on individual behavior in emergency situations. When individuals perceive that others around them are engaging in certain behaviors, they are more likely to adopt those same behaviors themselves. This can lead to the rapid spread of both positive and negative behaviors within a group. For instance, during a mass evacuation, if a group of people begins to panic and run, others may quickly follow suit, even if it is not the safest or most effective course of action. Hughes' influence code provides strategies for emergency responders to establish and promote positive group norms, such as calmness and cooperation, through clear communication and leadership.

Emotional contagion is another critical factor in group dynamics during emergency situations. When individuals are exposed to the emotions of those around them, they can quickly "catch" and adopt those same emotions themselves. This can lead to a rapid escalation of emotions within a group, from anxiety and fear to panic and chaos. Emergency responders must be aware of the emotional tone of a group and use empathic listening and strategic communication techniques to manage and regulate emotions, promoting a sense of calmness and stability.

Understanding these key factors in group dynamics is essential for emergency responders seeking to effectively manage and influence crowds in critical situations. By recognizing the complex interplay between social identity, norms, and emotional contagion, responders can develop targeted strategies to promote safe and constructive behaviors, reduce panic and confusion, and ultimately save lives. The application of Hughes' influence code in these situations provides a powerful tool for emergency responders to guide individuals toward safer decisions and promote more positive outcomes.

The complex interplay between social identity, norms, and emotional contagion in group dynamics can have significant consequences for emergency response efforts. For instance, during a natural disaster, a strong sense of community and shared identity can facilitate cooperation and collective action, enabling individuals to work together to overcome challenges and achieve common goals. However, this same sense of community can also lead to the emergence of norms that prioritize group loyalty over safety, causing individuals to engage in risky behaviors or resist evacuation orders.

Emergency responders must be able to recognize and adapt to these dynamic group processes. Hughes' influence code provides a framework for understanding and influencing group dynamics, emphasizing the importance of empathy, active listening, and strategic communication. By establishing trust and rapport with group leaders and influencers, emergency responders can promote positive norms and behaviors, such as cooperation and calmness, and reduce the spread of negative emotions like fear and panic.

The role of leadership in shaping group dynamics is also critical. During emergency situations, individuals often look to leaders for guidance and direction, and these leaders can play a significant role in establishing and promoting positive norms and behaviors. Emergency responders can work with group leaders to promote a sense of shared purpose and identity, and to establish clear expectations and guidelines for behavior. This can involve using persuasive communication techniques, such as storytelling and framing, to reframe the situation and promote a more positive and constructive mindset.

Effective management of group dynamics also requires an understanding of the social and cultural context in which emergencies occur. Different cultural groups may have distinct norms, values, and beliefs that influence their behavior during emergency situations. For example, some cultures may prioritize collective action over individual safety, while others may emphasize personal responsibility and self-reliance. Emergency responders must be aware of these cultural differences and adapt their communication strategies accordingly, using culturally sensitive language and approaches to promote cooperation and compliance.

The application of Hughes' influence code in emergency response situations has been demonstrated through various case studies and examples. For instance, during a recent wildfire evacuation, emergency responders used strategic communication techniques to establish trust and rapport with community leaders, promoting a sense of shared purpose and identity among evacuees. By framing the evacuation as a collective effort to protect the community, rather than a individual response to personal danger, responders were able to reduce resistance and promote cooperation, ultimately saving lives and reducing property damage.

In another example, during a mass shooting incident, emergency responders used empathic listening and active communication techniques to de-escalate tensions and manage emotions among witnesses and bystanders. By acknowledging the fear and anxiety of those present, and providing clear guidance and reassurance, responders were able to reduce panic and promote a sense of calmness, enabling individuals to provide critical information and assistance to emergency personnel.

These examples demonstrate the importance of understanding group dynamics in emergency response situations, and the effectiveness of Hughes' influence code in promoting positive outcomes. By recognizing the complex interplay between social identity, norms, and emotional contagion, and adapting communication strategies to the unique cultural and social context of each situation, emergency responders can save lives, reduce damage, and promote more constructive and resilient communities.

The Role of Stress and Anxiety in Human Behavior

Stress and anxiety are inherent components of crisis situations, significantly impacting human behavior. During critical moments, individuals' perceptions, decision-making processes, and actions are altered by the intense emotional and physiological responses triggered by stress and anxiety. Emergency responders must understand these dynamics to effectively manage and influence crowds or individuals.

Research at the National Crisis Institute has shown that stress and anxiety can lead to a state of heightened arousal, characterized by increased heart rate, blood pressure, and respiration. This physiological response prepares the body for "fight or flight," but it also impairs cognitive function, particularly in areas responsible for rational thinking and decision-making. As a result, individuals under stress may exhibit impulsive behavior, making rash decisions that can escalate situations or put themselves and others at risk.

Hughes' influence code recognizes the critical role of empathy in mitigating the effects of stress and anxiety. By acknowledging and validating individuals' emotions, emergency responders can establish trust and create a sense of safety, reducing the intensity of stress and anxiety. This approach enables responders to connect with individuals on a personal level, understanding their unique concerns and needs, and tailor their communication strategies accordingly.

The impact of stress and anxiety on human behavior is further complicated by the concept of "tunnel vision." When individuals are under extreme stress, their focus narrows, and they become fixated on the immediate threat or problem, neglecting peripheral information and potential solutions. This phenomenon can lead to a lack of situational awareness, causing individuals to overlook critical details or miss opportunities for de-escalation.

Effective management of stress and anxiety requires a deep understanding of human psychology and behavior. Emergency responders must be trained to recognize the signs of stress and anxiety, such as changes in body language, tone of voice, and speech patterns. By doing so, they can adapt their communication strategies to address the underlying emotional and psychological needs of individuals, rather than simply focusing on the surface-level symptoms of the crisis.

Real-world examples illustrate the importance of considering stress and anxiety in emergency response situations. During a recent hostage standoff, law enforcement officers used empathic listening techniques to establish a rapport with the hostage-taker, acknowledging his feelings and concerns. By doing so, they created a sense of trust and reduced the individual's stress levels, ultimately facilitating a peaceful resolution to the situation.

In another example, emergency responders used strategic communication techniques to manage the stress and anxiety of evacuees during a natural disaster. By providing clear, concise information and addressing individuals' specific concerns, responders helped to reduce panic and promote a sense of calmness, enabling evacuees to make more rational decisions and follow instructions.

These examples demonstrate the critical role of stress and anxiety in shaping human behavior during crisis situations. By understanding these dynamics and incorporating empathy and strategic communication into their response strategies, emergency responders can mitigate the effects of stress and anxiety, reducing the risk of escalation and promoting safer outcomes.

The interplay between stress, anxiety, and human behavior is complex, with each individual's response influenced by their unique experiences, personality, and coping mechanisms. Emergency responders must consider these factors when developing strategies to manage and influence crowds or individuals in crisis situations.

Hughes' influence code emphasizes the importance of active listening in reducing stress and anxiety. By attentively listening to individuals' concerns and responding empathetically, emergency responders can create a sense of trust and rapport, helping to mitigate the emotional intensity of the situation. This approach is particularly effective in situations where individuals feel overwhelmed or powerless, such as during natural disasters or terrorist attacks.

The concept of "emotional contagion" also plays a significant role in crisis situations. When individuals are exposed to others' emotions, they can "catch" those feelings, leading to a rapid escalation of stress and anxiety. Emergency responders must be aware of their own emotional state and take steps to manage their emotions, as this can help prevent the spread of negative emotions and promote a more calm and composed environment.

Effective communication is critical in managing stress and anxiety during crisis situations. Emergency responders must use clear, concise language, avoiding jargon or technical terms that may confuse or intimidate individuals. They should also be aware of nonverbal cues, such as body language and tone of voice, which can convey empathy and reassurance. For example, maintaining eye contact, using open and approachable body language, and speaking in a calm and gentle tone can help to reduce stress and anxiety.

The use of positive language and framing can also influence individuals' perceptions and behaviors during crisis situations. By focusing on solutions rather than problems, emergency responders can help individuals reframe their experiences and develop a more optimistic outlook. For instance, instead of saying "the situation is critical," responders might say "we are working to resolve the situation as quickly and safely as possible." This subtle shift in language can help to reduce stress and anxiety, promoting a more positive and resilient response.

Real-world examples illustrate the effectiveness of these strategies in managing stress and anxiety during crisis situations. During a recent mass casualty incident, emergency responders used active listening and empathetic communication to calm panicked individuals, providing clear instructions and reassurance to help them make informed decisions. By doing so, they reduced the risk of further injury or harm, promoting a more stable and secure environment.

In another example, law enforcement officers used positive language and framing to de-escalate a tense standoff situation. By focusing on the individual's concerns and needs, rather than their demands, officers were able to establish a rapport and build trust, ultimately resolving the situation peacefully. This approach demonstrates the importance of considering the emotional and psychological aspects of human behavior during crisis situations, rather than simply relying on traditional tactics or protocols.

By understanding the complex interplay between stress, anxiety, and human behavior, emergency responders can develop more effective strategies for managing and influencing crowds or individuals in crisis situations. Hughes' influence code provides a framework for responding to these situations, emphasizing the importance of empathy, active listening, and clear communication in reducing stress and anxiety and promoting safer outcomes.

Cognitive Biases and Heuristics in Crisis Environments

Cognitive biases and heuristics significantly impact human decision-making in crisis environments. Emergency responders must understand these psychological phenomena to effectively navigate complex situations and guide individuals toward safer choices. Hughes' influence code recognizes the critical role of cognitive biases in shaping human behavior, providing a framework for emergency responders to adapt their communication strategies and build trust with those in crisis.

In high-pressure situations, individuals often rely on mental shortcuts or heuristics to make rapid decisions. These cognitive biases can lead to systematic errors in judgment, causing people to misinterpret information or overlook critical details. For example, the availability heuristic can lead individuals to overestimate the likelihood of a particular outcome based on how easily examples come to mind, rather than actual probabilities. This bias can be particularly problematic in crisis situations, where accurate risk assessment is crucial.

The confirmation bias is another significant cognitive bias that affects decision-making in crisis environments. When individuals are under stress or pressure, they tend to seek out information that confirms their existing beliefs, rather than considering alternative perspectives. Emergency responders must be aware of this bias and take steps to present information in a clear, unbiased manner, encouraging individuals to consider multiple viewpoints and make informed decisions.

Anchoring bias is also a significant concern in crisis situations. When individuals are exposed to initial information or estimates, they tend to rely on these anchors, even if subsequent information suggests alternative solutions. Emergency responders can use this knowledge to their advantage by providing accurate, reliable information early in the crisis, helping to establish a positive anchor and guide individuals toward safer decisions.

The representativeness heuristic is another cognitive bias that can lead to errors in judgment. In crisis situations, individuals often judge the likelihood of an event based on how closely it resembles a typical case, rather than actual probabilities. Emergency responders must be aware of this bias and provide clear, data-driven information to help individuals make more accurate assessments of risk.

Real-world examples illustrate the impact of cognitive biases on decision-making in crisis environments. During a recent natural disaster, emergency responders used strategic communication to counteract the availability heuristic, providing accurate information about the likelihood of further hazards and encouraging individuals to take necessary precautions. By doing so, they helped reduce the risk of further injury or harm, promoting a more stable and secure environment.

Hughes' influence code provides a comprehensive framework for understanding cognitive biases and heuristics in crisis environments. By recognizing these psychological phenomena, emergency responders can adapt their communication strategies, build trust with individuals in crisis, and guide them toward safer decisions. The following sections will explore the application of Hughes' influence code in depth, providing evidence-based analysis and real-world examples to demonstrate its effectiveness in managing volatile situations.

Emergency responders must be aware of the cognitive bias known as the affect heuristic, which influences individuals' decisions based on their emotional state. In crisis situations, people often rely on their intuition, making decisions that align with their current emotional state rather than objective facts. Hughes' influence code recognizes this phenomenon and provides strategies for emergency responders to acknowledge and address the emotional aspects of decision-making.

For example, during a hostage situation, emergency responders can use empathetic communication to understand the emotional state of the individuals involved. By acknowledging their fears, concerns, and emotions, responders can establish trust and build a rapport that helps to de-escalate the situation. This approach allows responders to present alternative solutions that take into account the emotional aspects of the decision-making process, increasing the likelihood of a positive outcome.

The fundamental attribution error is another cognitive bias that affects human behavior in crisis environments. Individuals tend to overestimate the role of character and underestimate the impact of situational factors when explaining others' behavior. Emergency responders must be aware of this bias and avoid making assumptions about individuals' motivations or intentions based on limited information.

Instead, responders should focus on understanding the situational factors that contribute to an individual's behavior. By recognizing the impact of environmental factors, such as stress, fatigue, or lack of resources, responders can develop targeted strategies to address these underlying issues. For instance, during a natural disaster, emergency responders can provide clear information about available resources, such as food, water, and shelter, to help individuals make informed decisions about their safety.

The concept of framing effects also plays a significant role in crisis decision-making. The way information is presented can significantly influence an individual's perception of risk and likelihood of certain outcomes. Emergency responders can use this knowledge to their advantage by presenting information in a clear, concise manner that takes into account the cognitive biases of those involved.

For example, during a public health emergency, responders can frame messages in a positive light, emphasizing the benefits of taking preventive measures rather than focusing on the risks of not doing so. This approach can help to increase compliance with recommended protocols and reduce the spread of disease. By understanding the impact of framing effects on decision-making, emergency responders can develop effective communication strategies that promote safer choices.

Hughes' influence code provides a comprehensive framework for understanding cognitive biases and heuristics in crisis environments. By recognizing these psychological phenomena, emergency responders can adapt their communication strategies to address the emotional, social, and situational factors that influence human behavior. The ability to navigate complex decision-making processes and guide individuals toward safer choices is critical in emergency response situations, and Hughes' influence code offers a valuable tool for achieving this goal.

Real-world applications of Hughes' influence code demonstrate its effectiveness in managing crisis situations. Emergency responders who have incorporated the code into their communication strategies report improved outcomes, including increased cooperation from individuals in crisis, reduced conflict, and more effective management of resources. By providing a deeper understanding of cognitive biases and heuristics, Hughes' influence code enables emergency responders to make more informed decisions and develop targeted strategies that address the complex psychological factors at play in crisis environments.

Communication Breakdowns and Conflict Escalation

Communication breakdowns can escalate conflicts in crisis situations, posing significant risks to public safety. Emergency responders must be adept at navigating these complex interactions to prevent further violence or harm. Chase Hughes' influence code provides a framework for understanding the psychological factors that contribute to communication breakdowns, enabling responders to develop targeted strategies for de-escalation.

In high-stress environments, individuals often experience cognitive overload, leading to impaired decision-making and increased emotional reactivity. When coupled with inadequate communication, these factors can create a perfect storm of conflict escalation. Emergency responders who fail to recognize these warning signs may inadvertently contribute to the problem, exacerbating tensions and reducing the likelihood of a peaceful resolution.

Effective communication is critical in crisis situations, requiring emergency responders to be attuned to the emotional and psychological needs of those involved. Hughes' influence code emphasizes the importance of empathic listening, which involves actively engaging with individuals to understand their concerns and perspectives. By acknowledging the legitimacy of these feelings, responders can establish trust and create a foundation for constructive dialogue.

Strategic communication is also essential in preventing conflict escalation. Emergency responders must be able to articulate clear, concise messages that address the needs and concerns of all parties involved. This requires a deep understanding of the psychological and social factors at play, as well as the ability to adapt communication strategies to evolving situations. Hughes' influence code provides a structured approach to communication, enabling responders to navigate complex interactions with confidence and precision.

Real-world examples illustrate the importance of effective communication in crisis situations. During a recent hostage standoff, emergency responders used Hughes' influence code to establish a rapport with the perpetrator, ultimately securing the release of all hostages without incident. In another instance, responders employed strategic communication to calm a crowd of protesters, preventing a potentially violent confrontation.

By applying the principles of Hughes' influence code, emergency responders can reduce the risk of communication breakdowns and conflict escalation in crisis situations. This requires a commitment to ongoing training and education, as well as a willingness to adapt to emerging challenges and complexities. As the stakes continue to rise in critical moments, the ability to communicate effectively and build trust with individuals and crowds will become increasingly crucial for emergency responders.

The consequences of communication breakdowns can be severe, resulting in harm to individuals, damage to property, and erosion of public trust. Conversely, effective communication can save lives, prevent injuries, and promote a safer, more stable environment. By mastering the art of strategic communication and empathic listening, emergency responders can play a critical role in preventing conflict escalation and promoting peaceful resolutions in crisis situations.

Emergency responders must be aware of the role that emotional contagion plays in communication breakdowns. When individuals are exposed to stressful or traumatic events, their emotional states can become highly infectious, spreading rapidly to others in the vicinity. This phenomenon can create a ripple effect, escalating tensions and increasing the likelihood of conflict.

Hughes' influence code provides strategies for emergency responders to recognize and mitigate the effects of emotional contagion. By maintaining a calm and composed demeanor, responders can help to regulate the emotions of those around them, reducing the risk of escalation. This requires a high degree of self-awareness, as well as the ability to manage one's own emotional state in the face of adversity.

The concept of emotional contagion is closely tied to the idea of mirror neurons, which are brain cells that fire both when an individual experiences an emotion and when they observe someone else experiencing the same emotion. This neural mechanism allows humans to empathize with others, but it also makes us vulnerable to emotional contagion. Emergency responders who understand this phenomenon can use it to their advantage, employing empathy and active listening to build trust and de-escalate conflicts.

Effective communication in crisis situations also requires an understanding of the role that cognitive biases play in shaping human behavior. Biases such as confirmation bias, anchoring bias, and availability heuristic can lead individuals to misinterpret or distort information, increasing the risk of conflict escalation. Hughes' influence code provides strategies for emergency responders to recognize and overcome these biases, promoting more accurate and effective communication.

For example, during a recent crisis situation, emergency responders used Hughes' influence code to negotiate with a group of protesters who were demanding justice for a perceived injustice. By acknowledging the protesters' concerns and empathizing with their emotions, the responders were able to build trust and create a sense of mutual understanding. However, as the negotiation progressed, it became clear that some of the protesters were operating under the influence of cognitive biases, such as confirmation bias and anchoring bias. The responders adapted their communication strategy accordingly, using techniques such as reframing and open-ended questions to help the protesters re-evaluate their assumptions and consider alternative perspectives.

The use of technology can also contribute to communication breakdowns in crisis situations. Social media platforms, in particular, can amplify rumors and misinformation, creating an environment in which tensions can escalate rapidly. Emergency responders must be aware of these risks and develop strategies for mitigating them, such as using social media to disseminate accurate information and counter misinformation.

In addition to these factors, emergency responders must also consider the role that cultural and linguistic differences play in communication breakdowns. In today's diverse and globalized world, it is not uncommon for crisis situations to involve individuals from different cultural backgrounds or with limited proficiency in the dominant language. Hughes' influence code provides strategies for emergency responders to navigate these complexities, promoting effective communication and reducing the risk of conflict escalation.

By understanding the complex interplay of factors that contribute to communication breakdowns and conflict escalation, emergency responders can develop targeted strategies for preventing and mitigating these risks. The application of Hughes' influence code in crisis situations has been shown to reduce the risk of violence, promote peaceful resolutions, and save lives. As the complexity and unpredictability of crisis situations continue to evolve, the importance of effective communication and empathy will only continue to grow.

Chapter 3: "Building Rapport and Trust with Individuals in Distress"

Understanding the Psychology of Distress

Understanding the psychology of distress is crucial for emergency responders to build rapport and trust with individuals in crisis situations. The National Crisis Institute's research highlights that distressed individuals often experience a heightened state of emotional arousal, characterized by increased anxiety, fear, and agitation. This emotional state can significantly impair an individual's ability to process information, make rational decisions, and respond to verbal cues.

Hughes' influence code emphasizes the importance of recognizing the physiological and psychological symptoms of distress, such as rapid breathing, elevated heart rate, and constricted peripheral vision. By acknowledging these signs, emergency responders can adapt their communication strategy to meet the individual's needs, using calm and composed language to reduce emotional arousal and create a sense of safety.

The psychology of distress also reveals that individuals in crisis situations often experience a narrowed attentional focus, prioritizing immediate threats over long-term consequences. This phenomenon, known as "tunnel vision," can lead individuals to make impulsive decisions, increasing the risk of harm to themselves or others. Emergency responders trained in Hughes' influence code can use this knowledge to their advantage, employing targeted communication techniques to broaden the individual's attentional focus and encourage more rational decision-making.

Effective crisis communication requires an understanding of the complex interplay between emotional, cognitive, and environmental factors that contribute to an individual's distress. By recognizing the psychological and physiological mechanisms underlying distressed behavior, emergency responders can develop tailored strategies to build trust, reduce tension, and guide individuals toward safer decisions. The influence code provides a framework for responders to navigate these complex dynamics, leveraging evidence-based techniques to de-escalate conflicts and promote positive outcomes in high-pressure situations.

Research conducted by the National Crisis Institute has consistently shown that emergency responders who receive training in Hughes' influence code demonstrate improved crisis communication skills, resulting in reduced conflict escalation and increased cooperation from individuals in distress. These findings underscore the critical role that psychological insight plays in effective crisis management, highlighting the need for emergency responders to develop a deep understanding of the psychology of distress and its implications for building rapport and trust in high-stakes situations.

The psychology of distress also reveals that individuals in crisis situations often experience a significant imbalance in their brain's emotional and rational processing centers. The amygdala, responsible for processing emotions, can override the prefrontal cortex, which regulates rational decision-making. This imbalance can lead to impulsive behavior, as the individual prioritizes short-term emotional relief over long-term consequences.

Hughes' influence code provides emergency responders with strategies to recognize and address this imbalance. By using calm, empathetic language, responders can help regulate the individual's emotional state, reducing the amygdala's dominance and allowing the prefrontal cortex to reassert control. This approach enables individuals to regain a sense of rational perspective, making them more receptive to responder guidance and direction.

A critical aspect of understanding distress is recognizing the role of cognitive biases in shaping an individual's perception of reality. In high-stress situations, people often rely on mental shortcuts, such as confirmation bias or availability heuristic, to make quick decisions. These biases can lead to misinterpretation of information, exacerbating the crisis situation. Emergency responders trained in Hughes' influence code learn to identify and mitigate these cognitive biases, using targeted communication techniques to present information in a clear, unbiased manner.

For example, in a hostage situation, an individual may be convinced that the only way to resolve the crisis is to confront the perceived enemy. However, this perception may be driven by confirmation bias, where the individual selectively seeks out information that supports their preconceived notion. A responder using Hughes' influence code would acknowledge the individual's concerns, while gently introducing alternative perspectives and facts to broaden their understanding of the situation. By doing so, the responder can help the individual recognize the potential risks and consequences of their actions, encouraging a more rational and collaborative approach to resolving the crisis.

The influence code also emphasizes the importance of considering an individual's personal and cultural background when assessing their distress. Cultural differences can significantly impact how people experience and express emotions, with some cultures emphasizing restraint and others encouraging open expression. Emergency responders must be aware of these differences to provide effective support and build trust with individuals in distress. By taking a culturally sensitive approach, responders can tailor their communication strategy to the individual's unique needs, increasing the likelihood of a positive outcome.

In addition to cultural background, an individual's past experiences and traumas can also influence their response to crisis situations. Emergency responders trained in Hughes' influence code learn to recognize signs of post-traumatic stress disorder (PTSD) and other trauma-related conditions, adapting their approach to address these underlying factors. By acknowledging the individual's unique history and emotional landscape, responders can establish a stronger rapport, fostering trust and cooperation in even the most challenging crisis situations.

Establishing Initial Contact and Building Foundations for Rapport

Establishing initial contact with individuals in distress is a critical moment in emergency response situations. The first few seconds of interaction can set the tone for the entire encounter, influencing the individual's willingness to cooperate and the likelihood of a positive outcome. Chase Hughes' Influence Code emphasizes the importance of a thoughtful and strategic approach to initial contact, recognizing that this early stage lays the foundation for building trust and rapport.

Emergency responders must be aware of the profound impact of their initial words and actions on individuals in crisis. A calm and composed demeanor can help regulate the individual's emotional state, reducing anxiety and creating a sense of safety. Conversely, a abrupt or confrontational approach can escalate tensions, reinforcing negative perceptions and making it more challenging to establish trust.

Hughes' influence code provides responders with evidence-based strategies for establishing initial contact, including the use of open and non-threatening body language, active listening skills, and empathetic verbal cues. By adopting a relaxed and approachable posture, maintaining eye contact, and using calm, measured tones, responders can create an environment conducive to trust-building.

The National Crisis Institute's research has shown that individuals in distress are more likely to respond positively to responders who demonstrate empathy and understanding. This can be achieved through the use of reflective listening techniques, such as paraphrasing and summarizing, which help to acknowledge the individual's concerns and validate their emotions. By doing so, responders can establish a connection with the individual, fostering a sense of mutual understanding and respect.

Effective initial contact also requires an awareness of the individual's cognitive state, including any potential impairments or biases that may influence their perception of the situation. Responders must be able to adapt their communication strategy to accommodate these factors, using clear and simple language to convey critical information and avoid confusion.

In high-pressure situations, such as hostage standoffs or mass evacuations, the importance of effective initial contact is amplified. A well-executed approach can help to de-escalate tensions, reducing the risk of violence and promoting a more cooperative response from individuals in distress. By applying the principles outlined in Hughes' Influence Code, emergency responders can increase their chances of success, ultimately saving lives and minimizing harm in critical moments.

Building on the foundation of effective initial contact, emergency responders must prioritize active listening to establish a deeper connection with individuals in distress. This involves maintaining focus on the individual's words, tone, and body language, while avoiding distractions and interruptions. By doing so, responders can gather crucial information about the individual's concerns, needs, and motivations, ultimately informing their approach to building rapport.

Hughes' Influence Code emphasizes the value of verbal and non-verbal cues in facilitating active listening. Responders should use nods, gestures, and open-ended questions to encourage individuals to share their thoughts and feelings. This helps to create a sense of safety and trust, allowing individuals to feel more comfortable opening up about their experiences and emotions.

A critical aspect of active listening is empathy. Responders must be able to understand and acknowledge the individual's emotional state, without necessarily agreeing with their perspective. This can be achieved through reflective summaries, which involve paraphrasing the individual's statements to ensure understanding and show that their concerns are being taken seriously. For example, a responder might say, "Just to make sure I understand, you're feeling overwhelmed by the situation and concerned about your safety?" This simple acknowledgment can help to diffuse tension and create a sense of mutual understanding.

The National Crisis Institute's research has highlighted the importance of cultural sensitivity in building rapport with individuals in distress. Responders must be aware of the individual's cultural background and adapt their approach accordingly. This may involve using culturally specific language or customs, or being mindful of non-verbal cues that may have different meanings in different cultures. By demonstrating cultural competence, responders can establish trust and credibility, increasing the likelihood of a positive outcome.

In addition to active listening and empathy, responders must also be aware of their own emotional state and potential biases. This involves recognizing the physical and emotional signs of stress, such as increased heart rate or feelings of anxiety, and taking steps to manage these responses. By maintaining a calm and composed demeanor, responders can project confidence and control, helping to reassure individuals in distress and reduce the risk of escalation.

The application of Hughes' Influence Code in real-world scenarios has yielded impressive results. For instance, in a hostage situation, a responder used active listening and empathy to establish a connection with the individual, ultimately persuading them to release the hostages without incident. In another example, a responder adapted their approach to accommodate an individual's cultural background, using culturally specific language and customs to build trust and resolve the situation peacefully.

By integrating these strategies into their practice, emergency responders can enhance their ability to build rapport and trust with individuals in distress, ultimately improving outcomes and saving lives. The Influence Code provides a valuable framework for responders to navigate complex and dynamic situations, ensuring that they are equipped to respond effectively and compassionately in the face of crisis.

Active Listening and Empathy in Crisis Situations

Active listening and empathy are crucial components of crisis management, enabling emergency responders to build trust with individuals in distress. Chase Hughes' Influence Code emphasizes the significance of these skills in high-pressure situations, where effective communication can mean the difference between resolution and escalation. By prioritizing active listening and empathy, responders can create a foundation for rapport-building, ultimately guiding individuals toward safer decisions.

In crisis situations, individuals are often overwhelmed by their emotions, making it challenging for them to process information and respond rationally. Active listening helps responders to acknowledge and understand these emotions, creating a sense of safety and validation. This involves more than just hearing the individual's words; it requires responders to attend to non-verbal cues, such as body language and tone of voice, to gain a deeper understanding of their emotional state.

The National Crisis Institute's research has shown that empathic listening can significantly reduce tension and anxiety in crisis situations. By acknowledging the individual's feelings and concerns, responders can create a sense of mutual understanding, which helps to establish trust and credibility. This, in turn, increases the likelihood of a positive outcome, as individuals are more likely to cooperate with responders who demonstrate empathy and understanding.

Hughes' Influence Code provides responders with practical strategies for active listening and empathy, including the use of open-ended questions, reflective summaries, and non-verbal cues such as nodding and maintaining eye contact. These techniques enable responders to engage with individuals on a deeper level, building trust and rapport in even the most volatile situations.

Real-world examples demonstrate the effectiveness of these strategies in crisis management. For instance, during a hostage standoff, a responder used active listening and empathy to establish a connection with the individual, ultimately persuading them to release the hostages without incident. In another example, a responder employed empathic listening to calm a panicked crowd during a mass evacuation, preventing further chaos and ensuring a safe resolution.

By mastering active listening and empathy, emergency responders can enhance their ability to manage crisis situations effectively, reducing the risk of escalation and improving outcomes. The Influence Code provides a comprehensive framework for responders to develop these critical skills, empowering them to guide individuals toward safer decisions in even the most challenging situations.

Effective active listening and empathy in crisis situations require responders to be aware of their own emotional state and potential biases. This self-awareness enables them to manage their responses, maintaining a calm and composed demeanor that helps to de-escalate tense situations. Hughes' Influence Code emphasizes the importance of emotional intelligence in crisis management, providing responders with strategies to recognize and regulate their emotions, ensuring they remain focused on the individual's needs.

The use of verbal and non-verbal cues is critical in active listening and empathy. Responders can employ open-ended questions to encourage individuals to share their thoughts and feelings, while also using reflective summaries to acknowledge and validate their concerns. Non-verbal cues, such as nodding and maintaining eye contact, can convey empathy and understanding, helping to establish trust and rapport. For example, during a crisis negotiation, a responder used active listening skills to identify the individual's primary concern – the safety of their family – and addressed this concern directly, ultimately resolving the situation peacefully.

Cultural sensitivity is also essential in active listening and empathy, as responders must be aware of the individual's cultural background and adapt their approach accordingly. This may involve using culturally specific language or customs, or being mindful of non-verbal cues that may have different meanings in different cultures. The National Crisis Institute's research has highlighted the importance of cultural competence in crisis management, demonstrating that responders who are sensitive to cultural differences are more effective in building trust and resolving crises.

Real-world examples illustrate the effectiveness of active listening and empathy in crisis situations. During a mass casualty incident, responders used empathic listening to comfort and reassure victims, reducing their anxiety and stress. In another example, a responder employed active listening skills to de-escalate a violent confrontation between two individuals, resolving the situation without resorting to force.

The Influence Code provides responders with a comprehensive framework for developing active listening and empathy skills, enabling them to manage crisis situations effectively and improve outcomes. By prioritizing these skills, emergency responders can build trust with individuals in distress, reducing the risk of escalation and promoting safer resolutions. As Hughes' Influence Code demonstrates, the art of active listening and empathy is critical in crisis management, requiring responders to be aware of their own emotions, use verbal and non-verbal cues effectively, and adapt to cultural differences. By mastering these skills, responders can become more effective in managing crises and saving lives.

Cultural Sensitivity and Awareness in Building Trust

Cultural sensitivity and awareness are critical components of building trust with individuals in distress. Emergency responders must be able to understand and adapt to the diverse cultural backgrounds of those they interact with, taking into account the unique values, beliefs, and customs that shape their perceptions and behaviors. Chase Hughes' Influence Code emphasizes the importance of cultural competence in crisis management, providing responders with the skills and knowledge necessary to navigate complex cultural dynamics.

Research conducted by the National Crisis Institute has highlighted the significance of cultural sensitivity in building trust and resolving crises. Studies have shown that responders who are culturally aware and sensitive are more effective in de-escalating tense situations and establishing rapport with individuals from diverse backgrounds. This is because they are able to communicate effectively, avoiding misunderstandings and misinterpretations that can escalate conflicts.

Effective cultural sensitivity requires responders to be aware of their own biases and assumptions, recognizing how these may impact their interactions with individuals from different cultural backgrounds. Hughes' Influence Code provides responders with practical strategies for managing their biases, including self-reflection, active listening, and empathy. By acknowledging and understanding the cultural nuances that shape an individual's behavior, responders can tailor their approach to meet the unique needs of each situation.

Real-world examples demonstrate the importance of cultural sensitivity in crisis management. During a riot response, culturally sensitive responders were able to de-escalate tensions by using culturally specific language and customs, reducing the risk of further violence. In another example, a responder's awareness of cultural differences helped to resolve a hostage standoff, as they were able to understand the motivations and concerns of the individual involved.

The Influence Code provides a comprehensive framework for developing cultural sensitivity and awareness, enabling responders to build trust and establish rapport with individuals from diverse backgrounds. By prioritizing cultural competence, emergency responders can improve outcomes in critical situations, reducing the risk of escalation and promoting safer resolutions. Hughes' proven methods, refined at the National Crisis Institute, offer a powerful tool for managing volatile situations and saving lives.

Cultural sensitivity training is a crucial component of Hughes' Influence Code, enabling responders to develop a deeper understanding of the cultural nuances that shape individual behavior. This training emphasizes the importance of active listening, empathy, and self-awareness in building trust with individuals from diverse backgrounds. By recognizing and adapting to cultural differences, responders can tailor their approach to meet the unique needs of each situation, reducing the risk of miscommunication and escalation.

The National Crisis Institute's research has identified several key factors that contribute to effective cultural sensitivity in crisis management. These include an understanding of cultural values and norms, awareness of power dynamics and privilege, and the ability to communicate effectively across cultural boundaries. Hughes' Influence Code provides responders with practical strategies for developing these skills, including scenario-based training and interactive exercises.

Real-world examples illustrate the impact of cultural sensitivity on crisis outcomes. During a response to a natural disaster, culturally sensitive responders were able to establish trust with affected communities by using local customs and language, facilitating the delivery of aid and support. In another example, a responder's awareness of cultural differences helped to resolve a conflict between individuals from different ethnic backgrounds, preventing further violence and promoting a peaceful resolution.

The Influence Code's emphasis on cultural sensitivity is closely tied to its focus on empathy and active listening. By prioritizing the needs and concerns of individuals in distress, responders can build trust and establish rapport, even in high-pressure situations. This approach is grounded in a deep understanding of human behavior and psychology, recognizing that individuals are more likely to respond positively to empathetic and culturally sensitive communication.

Hughes' proven methods have been successfully applied in a wide range of crisis scenarios, from hostage negotiations to riot responses. By integrating cultural sensitivity into their approach, responders can improve outcomes, reduce risks, and promote safer resolutions. The Influence Code's comprehensive framework for developing cultural competence provides a powerful tool for emergency responders, enabling them to navigate complex cultural dynamics and build trust with individuals in distress.

De-escalation Techniques for Aggressive or Resistant Individuals

De-escalation techniques are a critical component of Chase Hughes' Influence Code, providing emergency responders with the skills to manage aggressive or resistant individuals in high-pressure situations. These techniques are grounded in a deep understanding of human behavior and psychology, recognizing that individuals in distress often respond more aggressively due to feelings of fear, anxiety, or frustration.

The National Crisis Institute's research has identified several key factors that contribute to effective de-escalation, including active listening, empathy, and strategic communication. By prioritizing these elements, responders can reduce tension, build trust, and guide individuals toward safer decisions. Hughes' Influence Code provides a comprehensive framework for developing these skills, emphasizing the importance of remaining calm, composed, and focused in the face of aggression or resistance.

Real-world examples demonstrate the effectiveness of de-escalation techniques in managing volatile situations. During a response to a hostage standoff, a responder's use of empathic listening and strategic communication helped to establish trust with the perpetrator, ultimately leading to a peaceful resolution. In another example, a responder's ability to remain calm and composed in the face of aggression helped to de-escalate a potentially violent confrontation, preventing harm to all parties involved.

The Influence Code's emphasis on de-escalation techniques is closely tied to its focus on building rapport and trust with individuals in distress. By prioritizing the needs and concerns of these individuals, responders can create a safe and supportive environment, reducing the likelihood of aggression or resistance. This approach is grounded in a deep understanding of human behavior and psychology, recognizing that individuals are more likely to respond positively to empathetic and strategic communication.

Hughes' proven methods have been successfully applied in a wide range of crisis scenarios, from riots to mass evacuations. By integrating de-escalation techniques into their approach, responders can improve outcomes, reduce risks, and promote safer resolutions. The Influence Code's comprehensive framework for developing de-escalation skills provides a powerful tool for emergency responders, enabling them to manage aggressive or resistant individuals with confidence and effectiveness.

Effective de-escalation techniques require a deep understanding of the emotional and psychological factors that drive aggressive or resistant behavior. Chase Hughes' Influence Code provides responders with a comprehensive framework for recognizing and addressing these factors, including the role of stress, anxiety, and fear in escalating conflicts. By acknowledging and validating the emotions of individuals in distress, responders can create a safe and supportive environment, reducing the likelihood of further escalation.

The National Crisis Institute's research has identified several key strategies for de-escalating aggressive or resistant individuals, including the use of open-ended questions, active listening, and empathic communication. These strategies enable responders to build trust and establish rapport, even in high-pressure situations. For example, a responder might use an open-ended question to encourage an individual to express their concerns or feelings, such as "Can you tell me more about what's bothering you?" or "How are you feeling right now?"

Real-world examples demonstrate the effectiveness of these strategies in managing volatile situations. During a response to a riot, a team of responders used active listening and empathic communication to de-escalate a group of angry protesters, ultimately preventing further violence. In another example, a responder used open-ended questions to establish trust with a resistant individual, eventually persuading them to cooperate with authorities.

The Influence Code's emphasis on de-escalation techniques is closely tied to its focus on building rapport and trust with individuals in distress. By prioritizing the needs and concerns of these individuals, responders can create a safe and supportive environment, reducing the likelihood of aggression or resistance. This approach is grounded in a deep understanding of human behavior and psychology, recognizing that individuals are more likely to respond positively to empathetic and strategic communication.

Hughes' proven methods have been successfully applied in a wide range of crisis scenarios, from hostage standoffs to mass evacuations. By integrating de-escalation techniques into their approach, responders can improve outcomes, reduce risks, and promote safer resolutions. The Influence Code's comprehensive framework for developing de-escalation skills provides a powerful tool for emergency responders, enabling them to manage aggressive or resistant individuals with confidence and effectiveness.

Maintaining Boundaries and Managing Emotional Contagion

Maintaining boundaries and managing emotional contagion are critical components of building rapport and trust with individuals in distress. Emergency responders must be able to navigate complex emotional landscapes while maintaining their own emotional stability. Chase Hughes' Influence Code provides a framework for achieving this balance, emphasizing the importance of self-awareness, empathy, and strategic communication.

Effective boundary maintenance requires responders to recognize their own emotional limits and take steps to manage their emotional exposure. This includes developing strategies for coping with stress, anxiety, and secondary trauma, as well as establishing clear boundaries with individuals in distress. By prioritizing their own emotional well-being, responders can maintain the clarity and focus needed to provide effective support.

Emotional contagion, the phenomenon of "catching" emotions from others, poses a significant challenge for emergency responders. When responding to critical incidents, responders may be exposed to intense emotions such as fear, anger, or despair, which can compromise their ability to think clearly and make sound decisions. Hughes' Influence Code offers practical strategies for managing emotional contagion, including techniques for recognizing and regulating one's own emotions, as well as methods for creating emotional distance without compromising empathy.

Real-world examples illustrate the importance of maintaining boundaries and managing emotional contagion in emergency response situations. During a hostage standoff, a responder's ability to manage their own emotions and maintain clear boundaries enabled them to establish trust with the perpetrator, ultimately facilitating a peaceful resolution. In another example, a team of responders used strategic communication techniques to mitigate the spread of panic and anxiety during a mass evacuation, preventing further escalation.

The Influence Code's emphasis on boundary maintenance and emotional contagion management reflects a deep understanding of the complex emotional dynamics at play in emergency response situations. By providing responders with the tools and strategies needed to navigate these dynamics effectively, Hughes' methods empower them to build trust, establish rapport, and guide individuals toward safer decisions, even in the most volatile and unpredictable environments.

Chase Hughes' Influence Code provides responders with a range of strategies for maintaining boundaries and managing emotional contagion, including the use of emotional labeling, empathy, and self-regulation techniques. Emotional labeling involves acknowledging and validating the emotions of individuals in distress, which can help to reduce tension and create a sense of safety. By recognizing and accepting the emotions of others, responders can establish trust and build rapport, even in high-pressure situations.

The National Crisis Institute's research has identified empathy as a critical component of effective crisis communication. Empathy involves not only understanding the emotions and needs of individuals in distress but also communicating that understanding in a clear and compassionate manner. Hughes' Influence Code offers practical guidance on how to develop and express empathy in emergency response situations, including techniques for active listening, nonverbal communication, and emotional validation.

Self-regulation techniques are also essential for managing emotional contagion and maintaining boundaries. These techniques include strategies for recognizing and managing one's own emotions, such as deep breathing, self-reflection, and physical exercise. By developing greater awareness and control over their own emotions, responders can reduce their susceptibility to emotional contagion and maintain the clarity and focus needed to provide effective support.

Real-world examples demonstrate the effectiveness of these strategies in emergency response situations. During a mass casualty incident, a team of responders used emotional labeling and empathy to calm and reassure victims, reducing anxiety and promoting cooperation. In another example, a responder used self-regulation techniques to manage their own emotions during a high-stress negotiation, enabling them to remain focused and composed even in the face of intense provocation.

The Influence Code's emphasis on maintaining boundaries and managing emotional contagion reflects a deep understanding of the complex psychological dynamics at play in emergency response situations. By providing responders with the tools and strategies needed to navigate these dynamics effectively, Hughes' methods empower them to build trust, establish rapport, and guide individuals toward safer decisions, even in the most challenging and unpredictable environments. Effective boundary maintenance and emotional contagion management are critical components of successful crisis communication, and the Influence Code offers a comprehensive and practical framework for achieving these goals.

Chapter 4: "Effective Communication Strategies for Emergency Responders"

Verbal and Nonverbal Cues in Crisis Communication

Verbal and nonverbal cues play a critical role in crisis communication, influencing the outcome of emergency response situations. Effective use of these cues can defuse tension, establish trust, and guide individuals toward safer decisions. Chase Hughes' Influence Code emphasizes the importance of mastering verbal and nonverbal communication skills to achieve these goals.

In high-pressure situations, such as hostage standoffs or mass evacuations, responders must be able to convey empathy and authority through their words and actions. Verbal cues, including tone, pitch, and volume, can significantly impact the perception of a responder's message. A calm, composed tone can help to reassure individuals in distress, while a raised voice or aggressive language can escalate the situation.

Nonverbal cues, such as body language and facial expressions, also convey important information about a responder's intentions and emotions. Maintaining eye contact, using open and approachable body language, and displaying empathetic facial expressions can help to establish trust and build rapport with individuals in crisis. Conversely, crossing arms or legs, avoiding eye contact, or displaying signs of anxiety can undermine a responder's credibility and create mistrust.

The National Crisis Institute's research has identified specific verbal and nonverbal cues that are most effective in crisis communication situations. For example, using open-ended questions and active listening skills can help responders to gather critical information and build trust with individuals in distress. Similarly, maintaining a calm and composed demeanor, even in the face of extreme provocation, can help to de-escalate tense situations and reduce the risk of violence.

By mastering verbal and nonverbal communication skills, emergency responders can improve their ability to manage crisis situations effectively. The Influence Code provides a comprehensive framework for developing these skills, drawing on real-world examples and evidence-based research to inform its approach. By applying these principles, responders can enhance their ability to communicate effectively in high-pressure situations, ultimately saving lives and reducing the risk of harm to themselves and others.

Effective use of verbal and nonverbal cues in crisis communication requires a deep understanding of the psychological dynamics at play. Responders must be able to read the emotional state of individuals in distress and adapt their communication approach accordingly. This involves recognizing subtle changes in body language, tone, and language patterns that can indicate escalating tension or potential violence.

Chase Hughes' Influence Code provides responders with a range of strategies for managing these complex interactions. For example, using "emotional labeling" techniques can help to acknowledge and validate the emotions of individuals in crisis, reducing tension and creating a sense of safety. This involves identifying and reflecting back the emotional state of the individual, such as saying "I can see that you're feeling really upset right now" or "You seem to be getting frustrated."

Nonverbal cues can also be used to reinforce verbal messages and build trust with individuals in distress. Maintaining a calm and composed demeanor, even in the face of extreme provocation, can help to de-escalate tense situations and reduce the risk of violence. This involves managing one's own emotional state through techniques such as deep breathing, self-reflection, and physical exercise.

The National Crisis Institute's research has identified specific nonverbal cues that are most effective in crisis communication situations. For example, using open and approachable body language, such as uncrossing arms or standing with an open posture, can help to establish trust and build rapport with individuals in crisis. Similarly, displaying empathetic facial expressions, such as a concerned or supportive look, can help to convey a sense of understanding and validation.

Real-world examples illustrate the effectiveness of these strategies in crisis communication situations. For instance, during a hostage standoff, a responder used emotional labeling techniques to acknowledge the emotions of the hostage-taker, saying "I understand that you're feeling desperate and scared right now." This helped to reduce tension and create a sense of safety, ultimately leading to a peaceful resolution of the situation.

In another example, a responder used nonverbal cues to de-escalate a tense situation with an individual who was experiencing a mental health crisis. By maintaining a calm and composed demeanor, using open and approachable body language, and displaying empathetic facial expressions, the responder was able to build trust with the individual and reduce the risk of violence.

By mastering verbal and nonverbal communication skills, emergency responders can improve their ability to manage crisis situations effectively. The Influence Code provides a comprehensive framework for developing these skills, drawing on real-world examples and evidence-based research to inform its approach. By applying these principles, responders can enhance their ability to communicate effectively in high-pressure situations, ultimately saving lives and reducing the risk of harm to themselves and others.

Active Listening and Emotional Intelligence in Emergency Response

Active listening and emotional intelligence are critical components of effective communication in emergency response situations. Chase Hughes' Influence Code emphasizes the importance of developing these skills to build trust, defuse tension, and guide individuals toward safer decisions. In high-pressure situations, such as riots or hostage standoffs, emergency responders must be able to quickly establish rapport with individuals in crisis, understand their concerns and emotions, and respond in a way that de-escalates the situation.

Emotional intelligence is the foundation of active listening. It involves being aware of one's own emotions and those of others, and using this awareness to inform communication strategies. Emergency responders with high emotional intelligence can recognize subtle changes in an individual's emotional state, such as shifts in tone, body language, or language patterns, and adapt their response accordingly. This helps to prevent miscommunication, reduce tension, and create a sense of safety.

The National Crisis Institute's research has identified specific active listening skills that are most effective in emergency response situations. These include maintaining eye contact, using open-ended questions, and paraphrasing statements to ensure understanding. By using these techniques, responders can gather critical information, build trust, and establish a rapport with individuals in crisis. For example, during a mass evacuation, a responder used active listening skills to understand the concerns of a panicked individual, saying "Just to make sure I understand, you're worried about your family's safety?" This helped to calm the individual and provide reassurance, ultimately facilitating a safe evacuation.

Real-world examples demonstrate the effectiveness of emotional intelligence and active listening in emergency response situations. For instance, during a hostage standoff, a responder used emotional intelligence to recognize the hostage-taker's emotional state, saying "I understand that you're feeling frustrated and desperate." This acknowledgment helped to reduce tension and create a sense of understanding, ultimately leading to a peaceful resolution of the situation.

The Influence Code provides a comprehensive framework for developing active listening and emotional intelligence skills in emergency responders. By applying these principles, responders can enhance their ability to communicate effectively in high-pressure situations, build trust with individuals in crisis, and guide them toward safer decisions. This is critical in emergency response situations, where lives are often at stake and every second counts.

Effective application of active listening and emotional intelligence in emergency response requires a nuanced understanding of human behavior and psychology. Chase Hughes' Influence Code provides responders with a range of strategies to manage complex interactions, including recognizing subtle changes in body language, tone, and language patterns that can indicate escalating tension or potential violence.

For instance, during a riot, a responder used active listening skills to understand the concerns of a protest leader, saying "I hear you're frustrated about the lack of action from authorities." This acknowledgment helped to diffuse tension and create a sense of understanding, ultimately leading to a peaceful resolution of the situation. The responder's ability to recognize and respond to the emotional state of the protest leader was critical in preventing further escalation.

The National Crisis Institute's research has also highlighted the importance of empathy in emergency response situations. Empathy involves not only understanding but also sharing the feelings of others. When responders demonstrate empathy, individuals in crisis are more likely to trust them and follow their instructions. For example, during a mass evacuation, a responder used empathetic language to reassure a panicked individual, saying "I know it's scary, but we're here to help you get to safety." This helped to calm the individual and facilitate a safe evacuation.

In addition to active listening and empathy, responders must also be aware of their own emotional state and how it may impact their interactions with individuals in crisis. Self-awareness is critical in emergency response situations, as it enables responders to manage their own emotions and respond in a way that is calm, composed, and professional. The Influence Code provides responders with strategies to develop self-awareness, including recognizing personal biases and triggers, and using techniques such as deep breathing and mindfulness to manage stress.

Real-world examples demonstrate the effectiveness of active listening, emotional intelligence, and empathy in emergency response situations. For instance, during a hostage standoff, a responder used a combination of active listening and empathy to establish a rapport with the hostage-taker, saying "I understand that you're feeling desperate and want to be heard." This acknowledgment helped to reduce tension and create a sense of understanding, ultimately leading to a peaceful resolution of the situation.

By applying the principles of active listening, emotional intelligence, and empathy, emergency responders can enhance their ability to communicate effectively in high-pressure situations, build trust with individuals in crisis, and guide them toward safer decisions. The Influence Code provides a comprehensive framework for developing these skills, enabling responders to respond to emergencies in a way that is calm, composed, and professional.

Building Rapport and Trust with Individuals in Distress

Building rapport and trust with individuals in distress is a critical component of effective communication in emergency response situations. Chase Hughes' Influence Code emphasizes the importance of establishing a connection with individuals in crisis, as this can significantly impact the outcome of the situation. In high-pressure scenarios such as riots or hostage standoffs, emergency responders must be able to quickly build trust with individuals who may be experiencing extreme emotional distress.

The National Crisis Institute's research has identified key strategies for building rapport and trust in emergency response situations. These include using open-ended questions, active listening, and empathetic language to create a sense of understanding and connection. By using these techniques, responders can establish a rapport with individuals in distress, reducing tension and creating an environment conducive to safer decision-making.

For example, during a mass evacuation, a responder used empathetic language to reassure a panicked individual, saying "I'm here to help you get to safety." This simple statement helped to calm the individual and establish trust, ultimately facilitating a safe evacuation. The responder's ability to recognize and respond to the emotional state of the individual was critical in preventing further escalation.

The Influence Code provides responders with a range of tools and techniques to build rapport and trust in emergency response situations. These include strategies for recognizing and responding to nonverbal cues, such as body language and tone of voice, as well as techniques for managing one's own emotional state to maintain a calm and composed demeanor. By applying these principles, responders can enhance their ability to communicate effectively with individuals in distress, reducing the risk of miscommunication and promoting safer outcomes.

Real-world examples demonstrate the effectiveness of building rapport and trust in emergency response situations. For instance, during a hostage standoff, a responder used active listening and empathetic language to establish a connection with the hostage-taker, saying "I understand that you're feeling desperate and want to be heard." This acknowledgment helped to reduce tension and create a sense of understanding, ultimately leading to a peaceful resolution of the situation. The Influence Code provides a comprehensive framework for building rapport and trust in emergency response situations, enabling responders to respond to critical moments with confidence and effectiveness.

Effective rapport-building in emergency response situations requires a deep understanding of human psychology and behavior. Chase Hughes' Influence Code provides responders with a framework for establishing trust and connection with individuals in distress, even in the most high-pressure scenarios. By recognizing and responding to emotional cues, responders can create a sense of safety and calm, reducing the risk of escalation and promoting more positive outcomes.

The National Crisis Institute's research highlights the critical role of empathy in building rapport and trust. Responders who can demonstrate genuine understanding and compassion are more likely to establish a connection with individuals in distress, even if they are experiencing extreme emotional arousal. For example, during a riot, a responder used empathetic language to calm a group of protesters, saying "I understand that you're frustrated and want to be heard." This simple statement helped to reduce tension and create a sense of understanding, ultimately preventing further violence.

The Influence Code also emphasizes the importance of nonverbal communication in building rapport and trust. Responders who are aware of their body language and tone of voice can use these cues to create a sense of calm and safety, even in the most chaotic environments. For instance, during a hostage situation, a responder used open and relaxed body language to reassure the hostage-taker, creating a sense of trust and reducing the risk of escalation.

Real-world examples demonstrate the effectiveness of building rapport and trust in emergency response situations. During a natural disaster, responders used active listening and empathetic language to comfort survivors, providing critical support and reassurance during a time of extreme crisis. By applying the principles outlined in the Influence Code, responders can enhance their ability to communicate effectively with individuals in distress, promoting safer outcomes and reducing the risk of miscommunication.

The Influence Code provides a comprehensive framework for building rapport and trust in emergency response situations, enabling responders to respond to critical moments with confidence and effectiveness. By recognizing and responding to emotional cues, using empathetic language, and being aware of nonverbal communication, responders can establish trust and connection with individuals in distress, even in the most high-pressure scenarios. This expertise is critical for anyone managing volatile situations, and the Influence Code provides a valuable resource for responders seeking to enhance their skills and promote safer outcomes.

De-escalation Techniques for High-Pressure Situations

De-escalation techniques are critical components of effective communication in high-pressure situations. Emergency responders must be able to guide individuals or crowds toward safer decisions, often in the face of extreme emotional arousal or panic. Chase Hughes' Influence Code provides a comprehensive framework for de-escalation, refined through extensive research and training at the National Crisis Institute.

Hughes' approach emphasizes the importance of empathic listening and trust-building in de-escalating volatile situations. By actively listening to individuals in distress and acknowledging their concerns, responders can create a sense of safety and calm, reducing the risk of escalation. For example, during a hostage standoff, a responder used empathetic language to reassure the hostage-taker, saying "I'm here to listen and help you find a peaceful resolution." This simple statement helped to reduce tension and create a sense of trust, ultimately leading to a successful outcome.

The Influence Code also highlights the role of strategic communication in de-escalation. Responders must be able to communicate clearly and effectively, using language that is calm, concise, and easy to understand. This requires a deep understanding of human psychology and behavior, as well as the ability to adapt communication strategies to meet the needs of diverse individuals and situations. During a mass evacuation, for instance, responders used simple, direct language to guide panicked individuals to safety, reducing confusion and promoting a more orderly exit.

Real-world examples demonstrate the effectiveness of Hughes' de-escalation techniques in high-pressure situations. In one notable case, a responder used active listening and empathetic language to calm a group of rioters, creating a sense of trust and reducing the risk of violence. By applying the principles outlined in the Influence Code, responders can enhance their ability to de-escalate volatile situations, promoting safer outcomes and reducing the risk of harm to themselves and others.

Effective de-escalation requires a combination of skills, including empathic listening, trust-building, and strategic communication. The Influence Code provides emergency responders with a proven framework for de-escalating high-pressure situations, empowering them to guide individuals or crowds toward safer decisions and promote more positive outcomes. By mastering these techniques, responders can reduce the risk of escalation and create a safer environment for everyone involved.

De-escalation techniques in high-pressure situations require a nuanced understanding of human behavior and psychology. Chase Hughes' Influence Code provides emergency responders with a comprehensive framework for de-escalating volatile situations, emphasizing the importance of adaptability and creative problem-solving. Responders must be able to think critically and respond effectively in dynamic environments, often with limited information and high stakes.

The Influence Code highlights the role of nonverbal communication in de-escalation, including body language, tone of voice, and facial expressions. Responders must be aware of their own nonverbal cues, as well as those of the individuals they are interacting with, to avoid escalating the situation. For example, maintaining a calm and composed demeanor can help to reduce tension and create a sense of safety, while aggressive or confrontational body language can exacerbate the situation.

Effective de-escalation also requires a deep understanding of the underlying causes of the crisis. Responders must be able to identify the root causes of the individual's or group's behavior, whether it be fear, anger, or desperation, and develop strategies to address these underlying issues. This may involve active listening, empathy, and creative problem-solving to find solutions that meet the needs of all parties involved.

Real-world examples illustrate the effectiveness of Hughes' de-escalation techniques in high-pressure situations. In one notable case, a responder used a combination of empathic listening and strategic communication to de-escalate a tense standoff between rival gangs. By acknowledging the concerns and needs of both groups, the responder was able to create a sense of trust and facilitate a peaceful resolution.

The Influence Code also emphasizes the importance of ongoing training and practice in de-escalation techniques. Emergency responders must be able to stay up-to-date with the latest research and best practices in crisis management, as well as continually refine their skills through hands-on training and simulation exercises. This ensures that responders are equipped to handle a wide range of high-pressure situations, from hostage crises to natural disasters.

By mastering the de-escalation techniques outlined in the Influence Code, emergency responders can reduce the risk of harm to themselves and others, promote more positive outcomes, and create a safer environment for everyone involved. The ability to think critically, respond effectively, and adapt to dynamic situations is critical in high-pressure environments, and Hughes' framework provides a comprehensive and effective approach to de-escalation.

Cultural Competence and Awareness in Emergency Communication

Cultural competence and awareness are critical components of effective emergency communication. Emergency responders must be able to navigate diverse cultural landscapes to build trust and facilitate safe outcomes. Chase Hughes' Influence Code emphasizes the importance of understanding cultural nuances and adapting communication strategies to meet the needs of diverse individuals and groups.

In high-pressure situations, cultural differences can exacerbate confusion and mistrust. Responders who are aware of these differences can tailor their approach to address specific cultural concerns, reducing the risk of miscommunication and escalation. For example, in a crisis situation involving a Muslim community, responders who are sensitive to Islamic customs and traditions can establish trust by respecting prayer times, dietary restrictions, and other cultural practices.

The Influence Code highlights the role of active listening in culturally competent communication. Responders must be able to listen attentively to individuals from diverse backgrounds, acknowledging their concerns and validating their experiences. This requires a deep understanding of cultural differences in communication styles, including verbal and nonverbal cues, tone of voice, and body language. By actively listening to and empathizing with individuals from diverse cultures, responders can build trust and create a sense of safety, even in the most volatile situations.

Real-world examples demonstrate the effectiveness of culturally competent communication in emergency response. In one notable case, a responder used cultural awareness to de-escalate a tense situation between law enforcement and a Native American community. By acknowledging the historical trauma and mistrust between the two groups, the responder was able to establish a rapport with community leaders and facilitate a peaceful resolution.

Hughes' approach emphasizes the importance of ongoing training and education in cultural competence. Emergency responders must be able to stay up-to-date with the latest research and best practices in culturally sensitive communication, as well as continually refine their skills through hands-on training and simulation exercises. This ensures that responders are equipped to handle a wide range of cultural scenarios, from language barriers to cultural differences in conflict resolution.

By mastering the principles of cultural competence and awareness, emergency responders can enhance their ability to communicate effectively in diverse cultural contexts. The Influence Code provides a comprehensive framework for building trust, establishing rapport, and facilitating safe outcomes in even the most challenging cultural environments.

Cultural competence in emergency communication requires a nuanced understanding of the complex power dynamics at play. Responders must be aware of their own biases and cultural assumptions, as well as those of the individuals they are communicating with. The Influence Code emphasizes the importance of self-awareness and introspection in developing culturally competent communication skills.

In situations where language barriers exist, responders can use visual aids, simple language, and nonverbal cues to convey critical information. For example, in a crisis situation involving a Spanish-speaking community, responders can use bilingual personnel or translation services to ensure that vital messages are communicated effectively. Additionally, responders can use culturally sensitive visual aids, such as diagrams or pictures, to facilitate understanding.

The role of cultural brokers is also critical in emergency communication. Cultural brokers are individuals who are familiar with the cultural nuances of a particular community and can facilitate communication between responders and community members. They can provide valuable insights into the cultural context of the situation, helping responders to navigate complex cultural dynamics and build trust with the community.

Hughes' approach highlights the importance of community engagement and partnership in developing culturally competent emergency communication strategies. Responders should work closely with community leaders and organizations to develop communication plans that are tailored to the specific needs of the community. This can include conducting cultural assessments, developing language-access plans, and establishing relationships with community-based organizations.

Real-world examples demonstrate the effectiveness of culturally competent communication in emergency response. In one notable case, a responder used cultural awareness to communicate effectively with a deaf community during a natural disaster. By using American Sign Language (ASL) interpreters and providing critical information in a visually accessible format, the responder was able to ensure that the deaf community received vital information and support.

The Influence Code provides a comprehensive framework for developing culturally competent communication skills in emergency response. By emphasizing the importance of self-awareness, cultural awareness, and community engagement, responders can enhance their ability to communicate effectively in diverse cultural contexts. Effective cultural competence in emergency communication is critical to building trust, establishing rapport, and facilitating safe outcomes in even the most challenging situations.

Technology-Based Communication Strategies for Emergency Responders

Technology plays a vital role in enhancing communication strategies for emergency responders. The Influence Code recognizes the potential of technology to amplify persuasive messaging, facilitate information sharing, and streamline crisis management. Emergency responders can leverage social media platforms, mobile apps, and digital alert systems to disseminate critical information quickly and efficiently.

In high-pressure situations, every second counts. Technology-based communication strategies enable responders to rapidly assess and respond to evolving situations. For instance, social media monitoring tools can help identify emerging trends, track public sentiment, and detect potential flashpoints. This allows responders to proactively address concerns, mitigate panic, and guide the public toward safer decisions.

Hughes' approach emphasizes the importance of integrating technology with traditional communication methods. By combining digital channels with face-to-face interaction, responders can create a robust and adaptive communication framework. This hybrid approach enables responders to reach a wider audience, build trust, and foster collaborative relationships with community members.

Real-world examples illustrate the effectiveness of technology-based communication strategies in emergency response. During a recent natural disaster, emergency management officials used social media to provide critical updates, instructions, and support to affected communities. By leveraging platforms like Twitter and Facebook, responders were able to reach thousands of people, providing timely information and reassurance during a period of intense uncertainty.

The Influence Code highlights the need for emergency responders to stay abreast of emerging technologies and innovative communication strategies. By embracing cutting-edge tools and techniques, responders can enhance their ability to persuade, inform, and protect the public in critical moments. Effective technology-based communication is essential for building trust, reducing confusion, and saving lives in emergency situations.

Emergency responders must consider the potential risks and limitations of technology-based communication strategies. Cybersecurity threats, technical failures, and information overload can compromise the effectiveness of digital communication channels. Hughes' approach emphasizes the need for responders to develop contingency plans, conduct regular system checks, and implement robust security protocols to mitigate these risks.

The use of data analytics is another critical aspect of technology-based communication strategies. By analyzing social media trends, response times, and community engagement metrics, responders can refine their communication approaches and optimize their messaging. This data-driven approach enables responders to identify areas for improvement, track the impact of their efforts, and make informed decisions about resource allocation.

Real-world examples demonstrate the value of integrating technology with traditional communication methods. During a recent mass evacuation, emergency management officials used a combination of social media, text alerts, and public address systems to provide critical instructions and updates to the affected population. By leveraging multiple channels, responders were able to reach a wider audience, reduce confusion, and facilitate a safer evacuation process.

Hughes' Influence Code highlights the importance of training and exercises in preparing emergency responders for effective technology-based communication. Regular drills and simulations help responders develop the skills and expertise needed to navigate complex digital landscapes, manage information flows, and make quick decisions under pressure. By investing in training and exercises, emergency management agencies can enhance their capacity to respond effectively in critical situations.

The strategic use of technology-based communication strategies can also facilitate collaboration and coordination among emergency response agencies. By sharing data, resources, and expertise, responders can create a unified and cohesive response effort, ultimately saving lives and reducing the impact of emergencies. The Influence Code provides a framework for emergency responders to harness the power of technology, build trust, and protect the public in critical moments.

Chapter 5: "Persuasion Techniques for De-escalating Violent Encounters"

Establishing Rapport in High-Stress Situations

Establishing rapport in high-stress situations is crucial for de-escalating violent encounters. Hughes' Influence Code emphasizes the importance of building trust and creating a connection with individuals or crowds in critical moments. This involves understanding the emotional and psychological dynamics at play, and using strategic communication techniques to diffuse tension.

In high-pressure situations, people are more likely to respond to emotional cues than rational arguments. Effective emergency responders recognize this and adapt their approach accordingly. By acknowledging and validating the emotions of those involved, responders can create a sense of safety and reduce aggression. This empathic approach is rooted in Hughes' proven methods, which prioritize building rapport and establishing a connection with individuals or crowds.

The National Crisis Institute's research highlights the significance of nonverbal communication in de-escalating violent encounters. Body language, tone of voice, and facial expressions can either escalate or diffuse tension. Responders who are aware of these nonverbal cues can use them to create a calming presence, which helps to reduce anxiety and aggression. By combining empathic listening with strategic nonverbal communication, responders can establish a rapport that fosters cooperation and reduces the likelihood of violence.

Real-world examples demonstrate the effectiveness of Hughes' Influence Code in de-escalating violent encounters. In one notable incident, a crisis negotiator used active listening and empathic responses to build a connection with a hostage-taker. By acknowledging the individual's concerns and validating their emotions, the negotiator created a sense of trust and ultimately secured the safe release of the hostages. This example illustrates the power of establishing rapport in high-stress situations, and highlights the importance of incorporating Hughes' Influence Code into emergency response strategies.

Hughes' approach recognizes that establishing rapport is not a one-size-fits-all solution. Each situation requires a unique blend of emotional intelligence, strategic communication, and cultural competence. By understanding these factors and adapting their approach accordingly, responders can create a tailored response that addresses the specific needs of the situation. This nuanced approach is critical for de-escalating violent encounters and saving lives in critical moments.

Building on the foundation of emotional intelligence and strategic communication, Hughes' Influence Code emphasizes the role of cultural competence in establishing rapport. Responders must be aware of the cultural nuances and values that shape an individual's perceptions and behaviors. By understanding these factors, responders can adapt their approach to create a sense of trust and connection with individuals from diverse backgrounds.

The National Crisis Institute's research highlights the significance of cultural competence in de-escalating violent encounters. In one study, crisis negotiators who received training on cultural awareness were more likely to successfully resolve hostage situations involving individuals from diverse cultural backgrounds. This underscores the importance of incorporating cultural competence into emergency response strategies.

Hughes' approach also recognizes the critical role of active listening in establishing rapport. By fully engaging with an individual's concerns and emotions, responders can create a sense of safety and reduce aggression. Active listening involves more than just hearing words – it requires a deep understanding of the underlying emotional and psychological dynamics at play. Responders who master this skill can diffuse tension and create a foundation for cooperation.

A notable example of the effectiveness of active listening in de-escalating violent encounters is the case of a police officer who responded to a domestic disturbance call. Upon arrival, the officer found a highly agitated individual who was threatening to harm himself and others. By using active listening skills, the officer created a sense of trust and connection with the individual, ultimately de-escalating the situation without resorting to force. This example demonstrates the power of Hughes' Influence Code in high-stress situations, where establishing rapport can be the difference between life and death.

The intersection of technology and crisis response also presents new opportunities for establishing rapport in high-stress situations. Social media platforms, for instance, can provide valuable insights into an individual's emotional state and motivations. By leveraging this information, responders can tailor their approach to create a sense of connection and trust. Hughes' Influence Code provides a framework for integrating technology into crisis response strategies, ensuring that responders stay ahead of the curve in de-escalating violent encounters.

Ultimately, establishing rapport in high-stress situations requires a deep understanding of human behavior, emotional intelligence, and strategic communication. By mastering these skills and incorporating Hughes' Influence Code into their approach, emergency responders can create a foundation for cooperation and reduce the likelihood of violence. The result is a safer, more effective response to critical incidents, where lives are saved and communities are protected.

Active Listening Strategies for Conflict Resolution

Active listening is a crucial component of Chase Hughes' Influence Code, enabling emergency responders to effectively manage volatile situations. By fully engaging with an individual's concerns and emotions, responders can create a sense of safety and reduce aggression. This approach is rooted in the understanding that people in crisis are more likely to respond to emotional cues than rational arguments.

Hughes' research at the National Crisis Institute has shown that active listening strategies can significantly de-escalate violent encounters. By acknowledging and validating an individual's emotions, responders can establish a connection and build trust. This empathic approach is critical in high-stress situations, where individuals may feel overwhelmed and disconnected from others.

The key to effective active listening lies in its ability to create a sense of psychological safety. When individuals feel heard and understood, they are more likely to cooperate and respond positively to persuasion techniques. Hughes' Influence Code provides a framework for responders to achieve this through verbal and nonverbal cues, such as maintaining eye contact, using open-body language, and employing a calm tone of voice.

Real-world examples demonstrate the effectiveness of active listening in conflict resolution. In one notable case, a crisis negotiator used active listening skills to establish a connection with a hostage-taker, ultimately securing the safe release of the hostages. The negotiator's ability to empathize with the individual's concerns and validate their emotions created a sense of trust, allowing for a peaceful resolution to the situation.

The science behind active listening also supports its use in emergency response situations. Research has shown that when individuals feel heard and understood, their stress levels decrease, and their cognitive functioning improves. This enables them to make more rational decisions, reducing the likelihood of violent behavior. By incorporating active listening strategies into their approach, responders can create an environment conducive to de-escalation and cooperation.

Hughes' Influence Code provides a comprehensive guide to active listening strategies, including techniques for verbal de-escalation, emotional labeling, and empathy-building. By mastering these skills, emergency responders can enhance their ability to manage critical incidents, reducing the risk of violence and promoting safer outcomes. The art of active listening is a powerful tool in the pursuit of conflict resolution, and its application in emergency response situations has the potential to save lives.

Hughes' Influence Code emphasizes the significance of verbal cues in active listening. Responders can use phrases such as "I understand" or "I hear you" to acknowledge an individual's concerns and show empathy. This verbal validation helps to create a sense of connection and trust, which is critical in de-escalating violent encounters.

Nonverbal cues also play a crucial role in active listening. Maintaining eye contact, using open-body language, and employing a calm tone of voice can all contribute to a sense of safety and rapport. Hughes' research has shown that individuals in crisis are highly attuned to nonverbal signals, and responders who can effectively use these cues can create an environment conducive to de-escalation.

The concept of emotional labeling is also a key component of active listening. By acknowledging and labeling an individual's emotions, responders can help to reduce their stress levels and create a sense of calm. For example, a responder might say, "I can see that you're feeling angry right now." This simple statement can help to validate the individual's emotions and create a sense of connection.

Real-world examples illustrate the effectiveness of emotional labeling in conflict resolution. In one case, a police officer used emotional labeling to de-escalate a situation with a violent suspect. The officer acknowledged the suspect's anger and frustration, saying, "I understand that you're feeling angry and scared." This simple statement helped to reduce the suspect's stress levels, allowing the officer to safely apprehend him.

Hughes' Influence Code also highlights the importance of empathy in active listening. Responders who can empathize with an individual's concerns and emotions are better equipped to create a sense of connection and trust. Empathy is not about agreeing with an individual's perspective, but rather about understanding their emotional experience. By using empathic statements such as "I can imagine how you'd feel in that situation," responders can create a sense of rapport and reduce the likelihood of violent behavior.

The application of active listening strategies in emergency response situations has been shown to have a significant impact on outcomes. Studies have demonstrated that responders who use active listening techniques are more likely to resolve conflicts peacefully, reducing the risk of injury or harm to all parties involved. By incorporating Hughes' Influence Code into their training and practice, emergency responders can enhance their ability to manage critical incidents and promote safer outcomes.

Verbal De-escalation Techniques for Crisis Management

Verbal de-escalation techniques are a critical component of crisis management, enabling emergency responders to diffuse tense situations and guide individuals toward safer decisions. Chase Hughes' Influence Code provides a comprehensive framework for verbal de-escalation, drawing on his extensive experience at the National Crisis Institute. This approach emphasizes the importance of trust-building, empathic listening, and strategic communication in reducing panic and confusion.

Effective verbal de-escalation begins with a deep understanding of human behavior in crisis situations. When individuals are under stress, their cognitive functioning is impaired, and they become more susceptible to emotional cues. Responders who can tap into this emotional landscape, using verbal cues to acknowledge and validate an individual's concerns, can create a sense of connection and trust. This trust is essential for de-escalating violent encounters, as it enables responders to influence an individual's decision-making process and guide them toward safer choices.

Hughes' research has identified several key principles of verbal de-escalation, including the use of calm and measured tone, active listening, and empathic statements. By speaking in a calm and measured tone, responders can help to reduce an individual's stress levels, creating an environment more conducive to rational decision-making. Active listening is also critical, as it enables responders to understand an individual's concerns and respond in a way that addresses their emotional needs.

Empathic statements are another powerful tool in verbal de-escalation, allowing responders to acknowledge and validate an individual's emotions. By using phrases such as "I understand you're upset" or "I can see why you'd feel that way," responders can create a sense of connection and rapport, reducing the likelihood of violent behavior. These statements do not imply agreement with an individual's perspective, but rather demonstrate an understanding of their emotional experience.

The application of verbal de-escalation techniques in real-world crisis situations has been shown to have a significant impact on outcomes. For example, in a hostage standoff, a responder who uses empathic statements and active listening can create a sense of trust with the hostage-taker, increasing the likelihood of a peaceful resolution. Similarly, in a riot situation, responders who use calm and measured tone, combined with strategic communication, can help to reduce tensions and prevent further escalation.

By mastering verbal de-escalation techniques, emergency responders can enhance their ability to manage critical incidents and promote safer outcomes. The Influence Code provides a proven framework for achieving this goal, drawing on Hughes' extensive experience and research in the field of crisis management. By applying these principles, responders can develop the skills and confidence needed to navigate even the most volatile situations, saving lives and reducing the risk of harm to all parties involved.

Verbal de-escalation techniques are highly dependent on the responder's ability to read and adapt to the situation. Hughes' Influence Code emphasizes the importance of situational awareness, allowing responders to adjust their communication strategy in real-time. This involves being attentive to nonverbal cues, such as body language and tone of voice, as well as verbal indicators, like an individual's words and phrases.

In high-stress situations, individuals often exhibit distinctive behavioral patterns. For example, a person who is agitated or angry may display rapid speech, raised tone, or aggressive posturing. Responders trained in Hughes' Influence Code can recognize these cues and adjust their communication approach accordingly. By mirroring the individual's verbal and nonverbal behaviors, responders can establish a sense of rapport and build trust.

Mirroring is a powerful technique in verbal de-escalation, as it allows responders to create a sense of connection with the individual. This involves subtly imitating the individual's speech patterns, tone, and body language, without being overt or insincere. By doing so, responders can establish a sense of mutual understanding, reducing the likelihood of further escalation.

Another critical aspect of verbal de-escalation is the use of open-ended questions. These questions encourage the individual to share their concerns and feelings, allowing responders to gather valuable information and build trust. Open-ended questions also help to slow down the conversation, reducing the likelihood of miscommunication and promoting a more rational exchange.

Hughes' Influence Code also emphasizes the importance of avoiding confrontational language or tone. Phrases like "You're wrong" or "That's not true" can escalate tensions and reinforce an individual's negative emotions. Instead, responders should focus on using neutral, non-judgmental language that acknowledges the individual's perspective without taking a confrontational stance.

The application of verbal de-escalation techniques in crisis situations requires extensive training and practice. Responders must be able to think critically and adapt quickly to changing circumstances. Hughes' Influence Code provides a comprehensive framework for developing these skills, drawing on real-world examples and case studies to illustrate the principles of verbal de-escalation.

In one notable example, a law enforcement officer used Hughes' Influence Code to de-escalate a potentially violent encounter with a mentally unstable individual. By employing active listening, empathic statements, and open-ended questions, the officer was able to establish a sense of trust and rapport with the individual, ultimately resolving the situation without incident.

The success of verbal de-escalation techniques in crisis management highlights the importance of effective communication in high-stress situations. By mastering these skills, emergency responders can reduce the risk of violence, promote safer outcomes, and build stronger relationships with the communities they serve. Hughes' Influence Code provides a proven framework for achieving this goal, offering a powerful tool for responders seeking to navigate even the most challenging crisis situations.

Nonverbal Communication Cues for Reducing Aggression

Nonverbal communication cues play a crucial role in reducing aggression during crisis situations. Chase Hughes' Influence Code emphasizes the significance of understanding and utilizing these cues to de-escalate violent encounters. Emergency responders must recognize that nonverbal signals can either exacerbate or alleviate tensions, depending on their execution.

Body language is a primary aspect of nonverbal communication, conveying emotions and intentions more effectively than verbal statements. In high-stress situations, individuals are more likely to react to nonverbal cues, such as posture, facial expressions, and proximity. Responders trained in Hughes' Influence Code learn to maintain a calm and composed demeanor, avoiding aggressive posturing that can escalate tensions.

Proximity is another critical nonverbal cue that responders must consider. Invading an individual's personal space can be perceived as threatening, leading to increased aggression. Conversely, maintaining a safe distance can help to de-escalate tensions and create a sense of security. Hughes' Influence Code teaches responders to respect personal boundaries and adjust their proximity accordingly.

Facial expressions are also vital nonverbal cues that can significantly impact the outcome of a crisis situation. A calm and empathetic expression can help to reassure individuals, while a confrontational or dismissive expression can exacerbate tensions. Responders must be aware of their facial expressions and ensure they convey a sense of understanding and concern.

Eye contact is another essential nonverbal cue that responders must master. Direct eye contact can be perceived as aggressive or confrontational, while avoiding eye contact altogether can be seen as dismissive or unengaged. Hughes' Influence Code teaches responders to maintain gentle, intermittent eye contact, conveying interest and attention without being perceived as threatening.

The use of open and relaxed body language is also crucial in reducing aggression. Responders should avoid crossing their arms or legs, which can be perceived as defensive or closed-off. Instead, they should maintain an open posture, with uncrossed arms and legs, conveying a sense of approachability and receptivity.

Hughes' Influence Code provides responders with the skills to recognize and adapt to nonverbal cues in real-time, allowing them to respond effectively to crisis situations. By mastering these nonverbal communication techniques, emergency responders can reduce aggression, build trust, and guide individuals toward safer decisions. The art of nonverbal communication is a critical component of Hughes' Influence Code, empowering responders to navigate even the most volatile situations with confidence and precision.

Effective use of nonverbal communication cues can significantly reduce aggression in crisis situations. Responders trained in Hughes' Influence Code learn to combine verbal and nonverbal techniques to create a cohesive de-escalation strategy. For instance, when responding to an agitated individual, a responder might use calm, slow speech while maintaining a relaxed posture and gentle eye contact. This multi-faceted approach helps to reassure the individual, reducing their perceived threat and creating an opportunity for constructive dialogue.

Paralinguistic cues, such as tone of voice and pitch, also play a critical role in nonverbal communication. A calm, gentle tone can help to soothe an agitated individual, while a loud or confrontational tone can exacerbate tensions. Hughes' Influence Code teaches responders to modulate their tone and pitch to match the situation, using a calm and reassuring tone to de-escalate aggressive behavior.

Nonverbal cues can also be used to redirect attention and create a sense of control. For example, a responder might use a subtle hand gesture to guide an individual away from a volatile situation, or use a calm, gentle motion to encourage them to sit down and engage in constructive dialogue. These techniques help to empower the individual, giving them a sense of agency and control over their environment.

The concept of "mirroring" is another powerful nonverbal technique used in Hughes' Influence Code. By subtly mirroring an individual's body language and facial expressions, responders can create a sense of rapport and understanding. This technique helps to build trust and establish a connection with the individual, reducing aggression and creating an opportunity for constructive communication.

In high-pressure situations, responders must be able to adapt their nonverbal cues quickly and effectively. Hughes' Influence Code provides responders with the skills to read and respond to nonverbal signals in real-time, allowing them to adjust their approach as needed. For instance, if an individual's body language indicates increasing agitation, a responder might adjust their proximity or tone of voice to de-escalate the situation.

Real-world examples illustrate the effectiveness of nonverbal communication cues in reducing aggression. In one notable case, a law enforcement officer used Hughes' Influence Code techniques to de-escalate a volatile standoff with an armed individual. By maintaining a calm demeanor, using gentle eye contact, and modulating his tone of voice, the officer was able to establish a connection with the individual and persuade them to surrender peacefully.

By mastering nonverbal communication cues, emergency responders can significantly reduce aggression and create safer outcomes in crisis situations. Hughes' Influence Code provides a comprehensive framework for understanding and utilizing these techniques, empowering responders to navigate even the most challenging situations with confidence and precision.

Managing Emotional Triggers and Empathy-Based Responses

Managing emotional triggers and empathy-based responses is crucial for emergency responders to effectively de-escalate violent encounters. Chase Hughes' Influence Code emphasizes the importance of understanding and managing one's own emotions to create a safe and calm environment. Responders must recognize their emotional triggers and develop strategies to maintain control, even in high-stress situations.

Emotional intelligence plays a significant role in this process. Responders with high emotional intelligence can better understand the emotions and needs of others, responding with empathy and compassion. Hughes' Influence Code provides responders with techniques to develop emotional awareness, recognizing the physical and psychological signs of stress and anxiety. By acknowledging and managing their own emotions, responders can create a sense of calm and stability, reducing the likelihood of escalation.

Empathy-based responses are critical in de-escalating violent encounters. Responders must be able to understand and acknowledge the perspectives and emotions of individuals in crisis. This involves active listening, asking open-ended questions, and providing reassurance without being confrontational. Hughes' Influence Code teaches responders to use empathic language, such as "I understand you're upset" or "I can see why you'd feel that way," to create a connection with the individual and reduce tension.

Real-world examples demonstrate the effectiveness of empathy-based responses in de-escalating violent encounters. In one notable case, a crisis negotiator used Hughes' Influence Code techniques to establish a rapport with a hostage-taker, acknowledging their concerns and providing reassurance. By creating a sense of trust and understanding, the negotiator was able to persuade the individual to release the hostages without incident.

The National Crisis Institute's research highlights the importance of emotional intelligence and empathy in emergency response situations. Studies have shown that responders who receive training in emotional intelligence and empathy-based responses are more effective in de-escalating violent encounters and reducing the risk of harm to themselves and others. Hughes' Influence Code builds on this research, providing a comprehensive framework for managing emotional triggers and developing empathy-based responses.

By understanding and managing their own emotions, emergency responders can create a safe and calm environment, even in the most volatile situations. Chase Hughes' Influence Code provides the tools and techniques necessary for responders to develop emotional awareness, empathy, and strategic communication skills, empowering them to guide individuals toward safer decisions and reduce the risk of harm.

Effective management of emotional triggers requires responders to develop self-awareness, recognizing the physical and psychological signs of stress and anxiety. Chase Hughes' Influence Code teaches responders to monitor their heart rate, breathing, and body language, making adjustments as needed to maintain a calm demeanor. This self-regulation enables responders to think more clearly and respond more strategically, even in high-pressure situations.

Empathy-based responses are equally critical in de-escalating violent encounters. Responders must be able to understand and acknowledge the perspectives and emotions of individuals in crisis, creating a sense of connection and trust. Hughes' Influence Code provides responders with techniques to active listen, asking open-ended questions and paraphrasing statements to ensure understanding. By acknowledging the individual's concerns and emotions, responders can reduce tension and create an opportunity for constructive dialogue.

The concept of "emotional labeling" is a key component of Hughes' Influence Code. This involves explicitly acknowledging and labeling the emotions of individuals in crisis, helping to reduce their intensity and create a sense of calm. For example, a responder might say, "I can see that you're feeling frustrated and angry right now." This simple statement can help to diffuse tension and create a sense of understanding, allowing the individual to feel heard and validated.

Real-world examples demonstrate the effectiveness of emotional labeling in de-escalating violent encounters. In one notable case, a crisis negotiator used Hughes' Influence Code techniques to establish a rapport with a suicidal individual, acknowledging their emotions and concerns. By creating a sense of trust and understanding, the negotiator was able to persuade the individual to seek help and avoid harm.

The National Crisis Institute's research highlights the importance of empathy-based responses in emergency response situations. Studies have shown that responders who receive training in empathy-based responses are more effective in de-escalating violent encounters and reducing the risk of harm to themselves and others. Hughes' Influence Code builds on this research, providing a comprehensive framework for managing emotional triggers and developing empathy-based responses.

In addition to emotional labeling, Hughes' Influence Code teaches responders to use "perspective-taking" techniques, which involve imagining oneself in the individual's situation and understanding their thoughts and feelings. This helps responders to develop a deeper understanding of the individual's needs and concerns, responding with empathy and compassion. By combining emotional labeling and perspective-taking, responders can create a powerful synergy that reduces tension and creates an opportunity for constructive dialogue.

By mastering these techniques, emergency responders can develop the skills and confidence needed to de-escalate violent encounters and reduce the risk of harm. Chase Hughes' Influence Code provides a comprehensive framework for managing emotional triggers and developing empathy-based responses, empowering responders to guide individuals toward safer decisions and create a more positive outcome.

Cultural Competence in De-escalating Violent Encounters

Cultural competence plays a vital role in de-escalating violent encounters. Emergency responders must understand the cultural nuances that influence an individual's behavior and decision-making process. Chase Hughes' Influence Code emphasizes the importance of developing cultural awareness, recognizing that cultural differences can significantly impact the outcome of a crisis situation.

Effective cultural competence requires responders to be aware of their own biases and assumptions, setting them aside to understand the individual's perspective. This involves developing an understanding of the individual's cultural background, values, and beliefs, and being sensitive to the power dynamics at play. By doing so, responders can establish trust and build rapport, creating a foundation for effective communication.

Hughes' Influence Code teaches responders to use culturally sensitive language and communication strategies, taking into account the individual's linguistic and cultural preferences. This includes using interpreters or translators when necessary, and being mindful of nonverbal cues that may be misinterpreted. By adapting their communication style to the individual's cultural context, responders can reduce misunderstandings and build trust.

Real-world examples demonstrate the critical role of cultural competence in de-escalating violent encounters. In one notable case, a crisis negotiator used Hughes' Influence Code techniques to establish a rapport with a hostage-taker from a culturally diverse background. By understanding the individual's cultural values and beliefs, the negotiator was able to build trust and persuade the hostage-taker to release the hostages safely.

The National Crisis Institute's research highlights the importance of cultural competence in emergency response situations. Studies have shown that responders who receive training in cultural competence are more effective in de-escalating violent encounters and reducing the risk of harm to themselves and others.

Hughes' Influence Code provides a comprehensive framework for developing cultural awareness, empowering responders to navigate complex cultural dynamics and create a more positive outcome.

Cultural competence is not just about understanding cultural differences; it's also about recognizing the impact of systemic injustices and biases on individuals and communities. Responders must be aware of the historical and social context that shapes an individual's experiences and perceptions. By acknowledging these factors, responders can develop a deeper understanding of the individual's needs and concerns, responding with empathy and compassion.

By mastering cultural competence, emergency responders can enhance their ability to de-escalate violent encounters and build trust with individuals from diverse backgrounds. Chase Hughes' Influence Code provides a powerful framework for developing cultural awareness, strategic communication, and empathic listening skills that are essential for managing volatile situations.

Building on the foundation of cultural awareness, responders must also develop an understanding of the individual's personal experiences and circumstances. Hughes' Influence Code emphasizes the importance of active listening, asking open-ended questions to gather information and understand the individual's perspective. By doing so, responders can identify potential triggers and develop a tailored approach to de-escalation.

Cultural competence in de-escalating violent encounters requires a nuanced understanding of power dynamics. Responders must be aware of their own position of authority and how it may impact the individual's behavior. By acknowledging and respecting the individual's autonomy, responders can reduce feelings of vulnerability and create a sense of safety. This involves using non-confrontational language and avoiding physical postures that may be perceived as threatening.

The National Crisis Institute's research highlights the critical role of cultural competence in reducing the use of force in emergency response situations. Studies have shown that responders who receive training in cultural competence are more likely to resolve crises peacefully, without resorting to physical intervention. Hughes' Influence Code provides a comprehensive framework for developing cultural awareness and strategic communication skills, empowering responders to manage complex and dynamic situations.

Effective cultural competence also involves being aware of the impact of technology on crisis situations. Social media, in particular, can play a significant role in shaping an individual's perceptions and behaviors. Responders must be aware of the potential for social media to escalate or de-escalate a crisis, and develop strategies to leverage technology in a way that supports de-escalation efforts.

In one notable example, a crisis negotiator used Hughes' Influence Code techniques to establish a rapport with an individual who was livestreaming a hostage situation on social media. By understanding the individual's motivations and using culturally sensitive language, the negotiator was able to build trust and persuade the individual to release the hostages safely. This example highlights the importance of cultural competence in navigating complex and dynamic crisis situations.

By integrating cultural competence into their de-escalation strategies, emergency responders can enhance their ability to manage violent encounters and reduce the risk of harm to themselves and others. Chase Hughes' Influence Code provides a powerful framework for developing cultural awareness, strategic communication, and empathic listening skills that are essential for effective crisis management. By adopting this approach, responders can create a safer and more positive outcome for all parties involved.

Chapter 6: "Influencing Group Dynamics in Emergency Response Scenarios"

Understanding Crowd Psychology in Emergency Situations

Crowd psychology plays a crucial role in emergency response scenarios, where the actions of a group can significantly impact the outcome. Emergency responders must understand the underlying factors that drive crowd behavior, including social influence, emotions, and environmental factors. Chase Hughes' Influence Code emphasizes the importance of recognizing these factors to develop effective strategies for managing crowds.

Research conducted at the National Crisis Institute has shown that crowds are often driven by a desire for safety and security. When individuals feel threatened or uncertain, they may turn to the group for guidance and support. This can lead to a phenomenon known as "emotional contagion," where the emotions of one individual spread rapidly throughout the crowd. Responders who understand this dynamic can use strategic communication to calm fears and reduce tensions.

The concept of social identity theory is also critical in understanding crowd psychology. When individuals identify with a particular group, they are more likely to adopt the group's norms and values. Emergency responders can leverage this phenomenon by appealing to the group's sense of shared identity and promoting behaviors that align with their values. For example, in a riot situation, responders might use messaging that emphasizes the importance of protecting the community and preserving social order.

Environmental factors, such as noise levels and visual stimuli, can also significantly impact crowd behavior. Loud noises and flashing lights can create a sense of chaos and disorientation, leading to increased aggression and anxiety. Responders who are aware of these factors can take steps to mitigate their effects, such as using calming music or reducing the intensity of lighting.

By understanding the complex interplay of factors that drive crowd psychology, emergency responders can develop targeted strategies for managing groups in emergency situations. Chase Hughes' Influence Code provides a comprehensive framework for analyzing crowd dynamics and developing effective influence strategies. By applying these principles, responders can reduce the risk of violence, promote cooperation, and ultimately save lives.

Emergency responders must also consider the role of leaders and influencers within a crowd. These individuals can significantly impact the group's behavior, often serving as a catalyst for either positive or negative actions. By identifying and engaging with these leaders, responders can harness their influence to promote calm and cooperation. For instance, in a mass evacuation scenario, responders might work with community leaders to disseminate critical information and encourage orderly exit procedures.

The National Crisis Institute's research has highlighted the importance of empathy and active listening in crowd management. When responders demonstrate a genuine understanding of the group's concerns and needs, they can build trust and establish a foundation for effective communication. This is particularly crucial in situations where cultural or linguistic barriers may exist. By using simple, clear language and avoiding technical jargon, responders can ensure that their message resonates with the crowd.

Technology also plays a significant role in shaping crowd dynamics, particularly in today's digital age. Social media platforms can rapidly amplify or mitigate tensions, depending on how they are utilized. Responders who leverage social media effectively can disseminate critical information, counter misinformation, and promote calming narratives. However, they must also be aware of the potential for social media to spread rumors or inflammatory content, which can exacerbate an already volatile situation.

A notable example of effective crowd management can be seen in the response to a natural disaster, where emergency responders used social media to provide regular updates on evacuation routes, shelter locations, and safety protocols. By doing so, they were able to reduce uncertainty and anxiety among the affected population, promoting a more orderly and cooperative response.

Chase Hughes' Influence Code emphasizes the importance of adaptability in crowd management. Responders must be prepared to adjust their strategies as the situation evolves, taking into account changes in the crowd's mood, size, and composition. This requires a deep understanding of the underlying psychological and social factors that drive crowd behavior, as well as the ability to think critically and make sound decisions under pressure.

By mastering these principles, emergency responders can develop the skills and expertise needed to effectively manage crowds in emergency situations. Whether it's a natural disaster, riot, or other critical incident, the ability to influence group dynamics and promote cooperation can be the difference between life and death.

Recognizing and Managing Group Polarization

Recognizing and managing group polarization is crucial in emergency response scenarios, where the stakes are high and decisions must be made quickly. Group polarization occurs when a crowd's emotions and beliefs become more extreme, leading to a heightened sense of urgency and decreased ability to consider alternative perspectives. This phenomenon can have devastating consequences, such as escalated violence or reckless decision-making.

Emergency responders must understand the underlying factors that contribute to group polarization, including social influence, emotional contagion, and cognitive biases. When individuals are part of a group, they are more likely to adopt extreme views and behaviors, especially if they feel a strong sense of identity with the group. This can lead to a snowball effect, where the crowd's emotions and actions become increasingly intense and difficult to control.

Research at the National Crisis Institute has shown that group polarization can be triggered by various factors, including perceived threats, social injustices, or charismatic leaders. In emergency situations, responders must be able to identify these triggers and develop strategies to mitigate their impact. This may involve using empathic listening skills to understand the crowd's concerns and values, and then crafting messages that address these underlying issues.

Chase Hughes' Influence Code provides a framework for managing group polarization, emphasizing the importance of building trust and establishing a rapport with the crowd. By doing so, responders can create a sense of safety and security, reducing the likelihood of extreme behaviors and promoting more constructive decision-making. This approach is grounded in evidence-based research, demonstrating that crowds are more receptive to influence when they feel heard and understood.

Effective management of group polarization requires a deep understanding of human psychology and behavior. Responders must be able to read the crowd's emotions and adjust their strategies accordingly, using techniques such as active listening, open-ended questions, and non-confrontational communication. By adopting this approach, emergency responders can reduce the risk of violence and promote safer outcomes in high-pressure situations.

Group polarization can be particularly challenging to manage in emergency situations where multiple factions or interest groups are present. In such cases, responders must navigate complex social dynamics, balancing the needs and concerns of different groups while maintaining a neutral and impartial stance. The

National Crisis Institute's research highlights the importance of cultural competence in these scenarios, as responders who understand the nuances of diverse cultural backgrounds can more effectively build trust and facilitate communication.

A notable example of successful group polarization management can be found in the response to a large-scale protest, where emergency responders employed a strategy of "layered communication." This involved establishing multiple channels of communication with different segments of the crowd, each tailored to the specific needs and concerns of that group. By doing so, responders were able to address the underlying grievances driving the polarization, reducing tensions and promoting a more peaceful resolution.

Chase Hughes' Influence Code emphasizes the value of flexibility and adaptability in managing group polarization. Responders must be able to adjust their strategies in real-time, responding to changing circumstances and evolving crowd dynamics. This requires a deep understanding of human behavior, as well as the ability to think critically and make sound decisions under pressure.

The use of technology can also play a critical role in managing group polarization, particularly in situations where social media is being used to mobilize or radicalize different groups. Emergency responders must be aware of the online landscape, monitoring social media platforms and other digital channels to identify potential flashpoints and develop strategies to mitigate their impact. By leveraging technology in this way, responders can stay ahead of the curve, anticipating and addressing emerging issues before they escalate into full-blown crises.

Ultimately, recognizing and managing group polarization requires a nuanced understanding of human psychology, social dynamics, and cultural context. By applying the principles outlined in Chase Hughes' Influence Code, emergency responders can develop the skills and strategies needed to navigate these complex scenarios, reducing the risk of violence and promoting safer outcomes in high-pressure situations. Effective management of group polarization is critical to maintaining public safety and preventing the escalation of emergencies into more severe and destructive events.

Strategies for De-escalating Tensions within Groups

De-escalating tensions within groups is a critical skill for emergency responders, as it can mean the difference between a peaceful resolution and a volatile, potentially deadly confrontation. The National Crisis Institute's research has identified key strategies that can be employed to reduce tensions and promote a more positive outcome. One of the most effective approaches is to establish a rapport with group leaders or influencers, who can then help to calm and direct their followers.

Building trust is essential in these situations, and responders must be able to communicate effectively with group members, taking into account their concerns, fears, and motivations. This requires a deep understanding of human behavior, as well as the ability to remain calm and composed under pressure. By actively listening to group members and acknowledging their perspectives, responders can create a sense of empathy and connection, which can help to diffuse tensions and reduce the likelihood of conflict.

Chase Hughes' Influence Code emphasizes the importance of non-verbal communication in de-escalating group tensions. Responders must be aware of their body language, tone of voice, and facial expressions, as these can convey just as much information as spoken words. By maintaining a neutral, open posture and avoiding aggressive or confrontational gestures, responders can create a sense of safety and reduce the perceived threat level, making it easier to establish a dialogue and resolve the situation peacefully.

The use of active listening skills is also crucial in de-escalating group tensions. Responders must be able to focus on the group's concerns, ask clarifying questions, and paraphrase their statements to ensure understanding. This helps to build trust and creates a sense of being heard, which can reduce feelings of frustration and anger. By employing these strategies, emergency responders can effectively de-escalate tensions within groups, reducing the risk of violence and promoting a safer, more positive outcome.

Effective de-escalation techniques also involve identifying and addressing the underlying causes of group tensions. This may involve resolving issues related to perceived injustices, addressing unmet needs or concerns, or providing alternative solutions to problems. By taking a proactive, solution-focused approach, responders can help to reduce tensions and promote a more constructive dialogue, ultimately leading to a more peaceful resolution.

De-escalation techniques must be tailored to the specific group dynamics and circumstances. For instance, in a hostage situation, responders may need to establish a rapport with the hostage-taker, while also addressing the needs and concerns of the hostages. This requires a nuanced understanding of the power dynamics at play, as well as the ability to communicate effectively with multiple parties.

The National Crisis Institute's research highlights the importance of cultural competence in de-escalating group tensions. Responders must be aware of the cultural norms, values, and beliefs that may be influencing the group's behavior, and adapt their approach accordingly. For example, in a situation involving a culturally diverse group, responders may need to take into account differences in communication styles, emotional expression, and conflict resolution strategies.

Chase Hughes' Influence Code emphasizes the value of flexibility and adaptability in de-escalating group tensions. Responders must be able to adjust their approach as the situation unfolds, taking into account new information, changing circumstances, and evolving group dynamics. This requires a high degree of situational awareness, as well as the ability to think critically and make effective decisions under pressure.

Effective de-escalation also involves managing the physical environment to reduce tensions and promote a sense of safety. This may involve creating a safe distance between group members, reducing noise levels, or providing a calm and comfortable space for dialogue. By controlling the physical environment, responders can help to reduce feelings of anxiety and stress, making it easier to establish a constructive dialogue and resolve the situation peacefully.

The use of technology, such as crisis negotiation teams and social media monitoring, can also play a critical role in de-escalating group tensions. These tools enable responders to gather intelligence, communicate with group members, and respond quickly to changing circumstances. By leveraging technology effectively, responders can enhance their ability to de-escalate tensions and promote a peaceful resolution.

Ultimately, de-escalating group tensions requires a combination of effective communication, cultural competence, flexibility, and situational awareness. By mastering these skills and adapting their approach to the specific circumstances, emergency responders can reduce the risk of violence, promote a sense of safety, and resolve complex situations peacefully.

The Role of Leadership in Shaping Group Dynamics

The Role of Leadership in Shaping Group Dynamics

Leadership plays a crucial role in shaping group dynamics during emergency response scenarios. Effective leaders can defuse tense situations, guide crowds toward safer decisions, and mitigate the risk of panic and confusion. Chase Hughes' Influence Code emphasizes the importance of leadership in influencing group behavior, highlighting the need for responders to develop strong trust-building, empathic listening, and strategic communication skills.

In high-pressure situations, such as riots or hostage standoffs, leaders must be able to think critically and make swift decisions that prioritize the safety of all individuals involved. This requires a deep understanding of human behavior, group psychology, and the factors that contribute to crowd dynamics. By recognizing the key influencers within a group and establishing a rapport with them, leaders can more effectively guide the crowd toward a peaceful resolution.

The National Crisis Institute's research has identified several key characteristics of effective leaders in emergency response scenarios. These include strong communication skills, emotional intelligence, and the ability to remain calm under pressure. Leaders who possess these qualities are better equipped to build trust with group members, address their concerns, and provide clear guidance during times of uncertainty.

Leadership styles can significantly impact group dynamics, with some approaches being more effective than others in de-escalating tensions and promoting cooperation. Autocratic leadership, for example, can exacerbate existing tensions by creating a power imbalance and suppressing individual autonomy. In contrast, democratic leadership styles that prioritize open communication, empathy, and collaboration are often more successful in building trust and fostering a sense of community.

By adopting a leadership approach that prioritizes empathy, active listening, and strategic communication, emergency responders can more effectively influence group dynamics and promote safer outcomes. This requires a nuanced understanding of the complex factors that contribute to crowd behavior, as well as the ability to adapt leadership strategies to meet the unique needs of each situation. By mastering these skills, leaders can play a critical role in shaping group dynamics and saving lives during emergency response scenarios.

Effective leadership in emergency response scenarios requires a deep understanding of the psychological and social factors that influence group behavior. Leaders must be able to recognize and respond to the emotional needs of group members, providing reassurance and support during times of uncertainty. This can involve active listening, empathy, and clear communication, as well as a willingness to adapt leadership strategies to meet the unique needs of each situation.

The National Crisis Institute's research has identified several key strategies for leaders to influence group dynamics in emergency response scenarios. These include establishing a strong presence, building trust with group members, and providing clear guidance and direction. Leaders who can effectively communicate their vision and goals, while also acknowledging the concerns and fears of group members, are more likely to build trust and foster cooperation.

Leadership decision-making is also critical in emergency response scenarios, where swift and effective decisions can mean the difference between life and death. Effective leaders must be able to quickly assess situations, weigh available options, and make informed decisions that prioritize the safety of all individuals involved. This requires strong critical thinking skills, as well as the ability to remain calm under pressure and think clearly in high-stress environments.

Real-world examples illustrate the importance of effective leadership in emergency response scenarios. For instance, during a natural disaster, a leader who can provide clear guidance and reassurance can help to reduce panic and promote cooperation among group members. Similarly, in a hostage situation, a leader who can establish a rapport with the perpetrator and build trust with the hostages can increase the chances of a peaceful resolution.

Chase Hughes' Influence Code provides a framework for leaders to develop the skills and strategies needed to effectively influence group dynamics in emergency response scenarios. By focusing on building trust, providing clear guidance, and adapting leadership strategies to meet the unique needs of each situation, leaders can play a critical role in shaping group behavior and promoting safer outcomes. Ultimately, effective leadership is essential for saving lives and reducing the risk of harm in emergency response scenarios.

Communicating Effectively with Diverse Groups
Communicating Effectively with Diverse Groups

In emergency response scenarios, effective communication is crucial for building trust, reducing panic, and promoting safer decisions. Emergency responders must be able to communicate effectively with diverse groups, including people from different cultural backgrounds, age groups, and socioeconomic statuses. Chase Hughes' Influence Code provides a framework for developing the skills and strategies needed to communicate effectively with diverse groups in high-pressure situations.

The National Crisis Institute's research highlights the importance of cultural competence in emergency response communication. Emergency responders who are aware of cultural differences and can adapt their communication style accordingly are more likely to build trust and establish effective relationships with diverse groups. This involves being sensitive to nonverbal cues, such as body language and tone of voice, as well as verbal cues, such as language and terminology.

Effective communication in emergency response scenarios also requires an understanding of the psychological and emotional needs of diverse groups. Emergency responders must be able to empathize with people who are experiencing fear, anxiety, or trauma, and provide reassurance and support during times of uncertainty. This involves active listening, clear communication, and a willingness to adapt communication strategies to meet the unique needs of each group.

The art of trust-building is critical in emergency response communication. Emergency responders who can establish trust with diverse groups are more likely to influence their decisions and promote safer outcomes. Trust-building involves being transparent, honest, and consistent in communication, as well as demonstrating a genuine concern for the well-being and safety of others.

Real-world examples demonstrate the importance of effective communication in emergency response scenarios. For instance, during a natural disaster, clear and concise communication can help to reduce panic and promote evacuation efforts. Similarly, in a hostage situation, effective communication between emergency responders and the perpetrator can increase the chances of a peaceful resolution. By developing the skills and strategies needed to communicate effectively with diverse groups, emergency responders can play a critical role in saving lives and reducing the risk of harm in emergency response scenarios.

Effective communication with diverse groups in emergency response scenarios requires a nuanced understanding of the complex factors that influence group behavior. Emergency responders must be able to recognize and respond to the unique needs and concerns of different cultural, social, and economic groups. This involves developing a deep understanding of the social and cultural context in which emergencies occur, as well as the psychological and emotional factors that drive human behavior in crisis situations.

The National Crisis Institute's research has identified several key strategies for communicating effectively with diverse groups in emergency response scenarios. These include using clear and simple language, avoiding technical jargon or complex terminology, and incorporating visual aids and nonverbal cues to facilitate understanding. Emergency responders must also be aware of their own biases and assumptions, and be willing to adapt their communication style to meet the unique needs of each group.

In addition to these strategies, emergency responders must also be able to navigate the complex power dynamics that often exist in emergency response scenarios. This involves recognizing and respecting the authority and expertise of community leaders, as well as being sensitive to issues of trust and credibility. By building trust and establishing effective relationships with diverse groups, emergency responders can increase the likelihood of successful outcomes and reduce the risk of conflict or miscommunication.

Real-world examples illustrate the importance of effective communication with diverse groups in emergency response scenarios. For instance, during a hurricane evacuation, clear and concise communication with Spanish-speaking communities can help to ensure that critical information is understood and acted upon. Similarly, in a hostage situation involving a mentally ill individual, effective communication between emergency responders and mental health professionals can increase the chances of a peaceful resolution.

By developing the skills and strategies needed to communicate effectively with diverse groups, emergency responders can play a critical role in saving lives and reducing the risk of harm in emergency response scenarios. This requires a deep understanding of the complex factors that influence group behavior, as well as a commitment to adapting communication styles to meet the unique needs of each group. By prioritizing effective communication and cultural competence, emergency responders can build trust, establish effective relationships, and promote safer outcomes in emergency response scenarios.

Building Trust and Cooperation in High-Stress Environments

Building trust and cooperation in high-stress environments is crucial for emergency responders. The ability to establish rapport with individuals or groups under duress can mean the difference between a peaceful resolution and a volatile escalation. Chase Hughes' Influence Code provides a framework for understanding the psychological and emotional factors that drive human behavior in crisis situations, allowing responders to develop targeted strategies for building trust and cooperation.

In emergency response scenarios, trust is often established through empathic listening and strategic communication. Responders who can actively listen to concerns, acknowledge fears, and provide reassurance can create a foundation for trust and cooperation. This involves being aware of nonverbal cues, such as body language and tone of voice, as well as verbal cues, like language and terminology. By adapting their communication style to meet the unique needs of each individual or group, responders can increase the likelihood of establishing trust and cooperation.

The National Crisis Institute's research highlights the importance of cultural competence in building trust and cooperation. Responders who understand the cultural nuances and values of the communities they serve can develop more effective strategies for establishing trust and cooperation. This involves recognizing the role of community leaders, respecting cultural traditions, and being sensitive to issues of power and authority.

Real-world examples demonstrate the effectiveness of Hughes' Influence Code in building trust and cooperation. For instance, during a hostage standoff, a responder who uses empathic listening and strategic communication can establish a rapport with the perpetrator, increasing the chances of a peaceful resolution. Similarly, in a mass evacuation scenario, responders who can provide clear and concise information, while also addressing concerns and fears, can reduce panic and promote cooperation.

By understanding the psychological and emotional factors that drive human behavior in crisis situations, emergency responders can develop the skills and strategies needed to build trust and cooperation. This requires a deep understanding of the complex factors that influence group dynamics, as well as a commitment to adapting communication styles to meet the unique needs of each individual or group. Through the application of Hughes' Influence Code, responders can increase the likelihood of successful outcomes and reduce the risk of harm in emergency response scenarios.

Establishing trust and cooperation in high-stress environments requires emergency responders to be adaptable and responsive to the unique needs of each situation. The ability to read social cues, recognize emotional triggers, and adjust communication strategies accordingly is critical for building rapport with individuals or groups under duress. Chase Hughes' Influence Code provides a framework for understanding these complex dynamics and developing targeted strategies for establishing trust and cooperation.

In high-stress environments, emotional contagion can play a significant role in shaping group behavior. When responders can recognize and manage their own emotions, they are better equipped to de-escalate tense situations and promote cooperation. This involves being aware of the emotional tone of the environment, recognizing emotional triggers, and using strategies such as empathy and active listening to reduce tension.

The National Crisis Institute's research highlights the importance of scenario-based training in preparing responders for high-stress environments. By simulating real-world scenarios, responders can develop the skills and strategies needed to establish trust and cooperation in a variety of contexts. This includes training on conflict resolution, crisis communication, and cultural competence, all of which are critical for building rapport with diverse groups.

Real-world examples demonstrate the effectiveness of Hughes' Influence Code in establishing trust and cooperation. For instance, during a riot control scenario, responders who use strategic communication and empathy can reduce tensions and promote de-escalation. Similarly, in a disaster response scenario, responders who can provide clear and concise information, while also addressing concerns and fears, can increase cooperation and promote community resilience.

By applying the principles of Hughes' Influence Code, emergency responders can develop the skills and strategies needed to establish trust and cooperation in high-stress environments. This requires a deep understanding of human behavior, emotional intelligence, and cultural competence, as well as a commitment to adapting communication styles to meet the unique needs of each situation. Through effective training and scenario-based practice, responders can increase their ability to build trust and cooperation, ultimately reducing the risk of harm and promoting successful outcomes in emergency response scenarios.

Chapter 7: "Managing Stress and Emotional Control in High-Pressure Situations"

Understanding the Psychological Impact of Stress on Decision-Making

Stress has a profound impact on decision-making in high-pressure situations. Emergency responders, like Ethan Slade, must be aware of the psychological effects of stress to make informed decisions that save lives. Research conducted at the National Crisis Institute reveals that stress can alter cognitive function, leading to impaired judgment and decreased reaction time. When individuals are under stress, their brains prioritize immediate survival over rational thinking, often resulting in impulsive decisions.

The body's stress response, also known as the "fight or flight" response, is triggered by the release of hormones like adrenaline and cortisol. These hormones prepare the body to respond to a perceived threat, but they also compromise the prefrontal cortex, the region responsible for rational decision-making. As a result, stressed individuals may rely more heavily on intuition and instincts, rather than careful consideration and analysis.

In emergency response situations, this can have devastating consequences. For example, during a hostage standoff, a stressed responder may be more likely to act impulsively, potentially escalating the situation and putting lives at risk. Conversely, a responder who can manage their stress and maintain a clear head is better equipped to navigate complex situations and make strategic decisions that promote a peaceful resolution.

Understanding the psychological impact of stress on decision-making is crucial for emergency responders. By recognizing the effects of stress on their own cognitive function, responders can develop strategies to mitigate its influence and make more informed decisions in high-pressure situations. This may involve techniques like deep breathing, mindfulness, or tactical pause, which can help reduce stress and promote clearer thinking. By mastering these skills, responders like Ethan Slade can improve their decision-making abilities and increase their effectiveness in critical situations.

The impact of stress on decision-making can be further understood by examining the role of emotional intelligence in emergency response situations. Responders with high emotional intelligence are better equipped to recognize and manage their own emotions, as well as those of others, in high-pressure situations. This enables them to make more informed decisions and communicate more effectively with individuals or crowds.

For instance, during a mass evacuation, a responder with high emotional intelligence can empathize with the fear and anxiety of the crowd, using this understanding to develop a communication strategy that reassures and calms the crowd. By doing so, they can reduce the risk of panic and chaos, creating a safer environment for everyone involved.

Research at the National Crisis Institute has shown that responders who undergo training in emotional intelligence and stress management demonstrate improved decision-making skills and reduced stress levels in emergency situations. This training enables them to develop coping mechanisms, such as tactical breathing and self-awareness, which help mitigate the effects of stress on their cognitive function.

Moreover, the concept of "situational awareness" is critical in understanding the psychological impact of stress on decision-making. Situational awareness refers to a responder's ability to perceive and understand their environment, including the people, objects, and events within it. When responders are under stress, their situational awareness can be compromised, leading to tunnel vision and a narrowed focus on a specific aspect of the situation.

To combat this, emergency responders can use techniques such as "threat assessment" and "environmental scanning" to maintain a broader perspective and stay aware of their surroundings. By doing so, they can make more informed decisions and respond more effectively to changing situations. Chase Hughes' influence strategies, as outlined in his Influence Code, provide a framework for responders to develop these skills and improve their decision-making abilities in high-pressure situations.

By combining emotional intelligence, stress management, and situational awareness, emergency responders like Ethan Slade can optimize their decision-making skills and perform more effectively in critical situations. This enables them to save lives, reduce risk, and promote safer outcomes in emergency response situations.

Recognizing and Managing Emotional Triggers in High-Pressure Environments

Emotional triggers can significantly impact an emergency responder's ability to manage stress and make effective decisions in high-pressure environments. These triggers can be personal, such as a traumatic experience, or situational, like a hostile crowd. When triggered, responders may experience a range of emotions, from anxiety and fear to anger and frustration.

Research at the National Crisis Institute has identified that emotional triggers can compromise a responder's ability to communicate effectively, think critically, and make sound judgments. For example, a responder who has experienced a traumatic event in the past may be more likely to react impulsively when faced with a similar situation, potentially escalating the situation rather than de-escalating it.

To recognize and manage emotional triggers, responders must develop self-awareness and understand their own emotional responses to different situations. This can be achieved through training and practice in emotional intelligence, which enables responders to identify and regulate their emotions, even in the most challenging environments.

Chase Hughes' Influence Code emphasizes the importance of self-awareness and emotional regulation in emergency response situations. By recognizing and managing their emotional triggers, responders like Ethan Slade can improve their decision-making skills, communicate more effectively, and build trust with individuals or crowds. This, in turn, enables them to guide people toward safer decisions and reduce the risk of conflict or harm.

Effective management of emotional triggers also requires an understanding of the physical and psychological responses that occur under stress. When responders are aware of their physical symptoms, such as a rapid heart rate or tense muscles, they can take steps to manage these responses and maintain control over their emotions. This enables them to stay focused, think clearly, and make informed decisions, even in the most high-pressure situations.

By developing an awareness of emotional triggers and learning strategies to manage them, emergency responders can optimize their performance and improve outcomes in critical situations. The next step is to explore the specific techniques and tools that can be used to recognize and manage emotional triggers, enabling responders to maintain emotional control and make effective decisions under pressure.

Developing strategies to manage emotional triggers is crucial for emergency responders like Ethan Slade. One effective approach is to practice mindfulness and meditation, which can help reduce stress and anxiety by teaching responders to focus on the present moment. This enables them to recognize their emotional triggers and take steps to manage them before they escalate.

For example, a responder who is aware of their tendency to become angry in high-pressure situations can use mindfulness techniques to acknowledge and regulate their emotions. By taking a few deep breaths and focusing on their surroundings, they can calm themselves and respond more thoughtfully to the situation.

Another key strategy is to develop a pre-response routine that helps responders prepare for high-pressure situations. This can include physical activities like stretching or jumping jacks, which can help reduce tension and increase focus. It can also involve mental preparation, such as visualization or positive self-talk, which can help responders build confidence and stay focused under pressure.

Chase Hughes' Influence Code emphasizes the importance of developing a personalized approach to managing emotional triggers. By understanding their individual strengths and weaknesses, responders can develop strategies that work best for them and improve their performance in high-pressure situations. This may involve seeking support from colleagues or mentors, who can provide guidance and feedback on their progress.

Effective management of emotional triggers also requires an understanding of the role of self-care in maintaining emotional well-being. Responders who prioritize self-care, including getting enough sleep, eating a healthy diet, and engaging in regular exercise, are better equipped to manage stress and anxiety. They are also more resilient in the face of adversity, which enables them to perform at their best even in the most challenging situations.

By combining these strategies, emergency responders can develop the skills and resilience needed to manage emotional triggers and perform effectively in high-pressure environments. This enables them to provide better support to individuals and communities in need, while also maintaining their own physical and emotional well-being. Ultimately, recognizing and managing emotional triggers is a critical component of effective emergency response, and one that can have a significant impact on outcomes in critical situations.

Developing Resilience and Coping Strategies for Emergency Responders

Emergency responders like Ethan Slade face unprecedented stress and pressure in their daily work. The National Crisis Institute's research highlights the critical need for resilience and effective coping strategies to manage these demands. Developing resilience is not just about withstanding adversity, but also about emerging stronger and more capable of handling future challenges.

Chase Hughes' Influence Code emphasizes the importance of proactive stress management and emotional control in emergency response situations. By acknowledging the physical and psychological toll of their work, responders can take steps to mitigate its effects and maintain their well-being. This includes recognizing the signs of burnout, such as fatigue, irritability, and decreased performance, and taking proactive measures to address them.

Effective coping strategies for emergency responders involve a combination of personal and professional techniques. On a personal level, responders can prioritize self-care activities like exercise, meditation, and social support to help manage stress and maintain emotional balance. Professionally, they can develop skills like critical incident stress management and peer support to help colleagues cope with traumatic events.

The Influence Code's approach to resilience development focuses on building emotional intelligence, empathy, and communication skills. By cultivating these qualities, responders can better navigate high-pressure situations and build trust with individuals and crowds. This, in turn, enables them to guide people toward safer decisions and reduce the risk of conflict or harm.

Research at the National Crisis Institute has shown that emergency responders who receive training in resilience and coping strategies demonstrate improved performance, reduced stress, and enhanced overall well-being. These findings underscore the importance of investing in responder wellness and providing them with the tools and support needed to thrive in their roles. By developing resilience and effective coping strategies, responders like Ethan Slade can optimize their performance, maintain their physical and emotional health, and provide better support to individuals and communities in need.

Emergency responders often face situations that test their emotional limits, such as responding to traumatic accidents or dealing with aggressive individuals. Developing resilience and coping strategies is crucial to managing these stresses and maintaining emotional control. Chase Hughes' Influence Code provides a framework for building resilience through techniques like mindfulness, self-awareness, and emotional regulation.

Mindfulness practices, such as meditation and deep breathing, can help responders stay focused and calm in high-pressure situations. By cultivating self-awareness, responders can recognize their emotional triggers and take steps to manage them before they escalate. Emotional regulation techniques, such as cognitive reappraisal and emotional labeling, can also help responders manage their emotions and respond more thoughtfully to challenging situations.

The National Crisis Institute's research has shown that emergency responders who receive training in resilience and coping strategies demonstrate improved performance, reduced stress, and enhanced overall well-being. For example, a study on crisis negotiation found that responders who received training in emotional intelligence and empathy were better able to de-escalate conflicts and resolve crises peacefully.

Effective coping strategies for emergency responders also involve building strong support networks, both personally and professionally. Responders can benefit from peer support groups, where they can share their experiences and receive support from colleagues who understand the stresses of their work. They can also prioritize self-care activities, such as exercise, socializing, and hobbies, to help manage stress and maintain emotional balance.

Chase Hughes' Influence Code emphasizes the importance of proactive stress management and emotional control in emergency response situations. By developing resilience and effective coping strategies, responders like Ethan Slade can optimize their performance, maintain their physical and emotional health, and provide better support to individuals and communities in need. The code's approach to building resilience is centered on empowering responders with the skills and knowledge they need to thrive in their roles, even in the most challenging situations.

The Role of Self-Awareness in Maintaining Emotional Control

Emergency responders like Ethan Slade face high-pressure situations that demand emotional control. Self-awareness is crucial in maintaining this control, as it enables responders to recognize their emotions and thoughts, and manage them effectively. The National Crisis Institute's research emphasizes the importance of self-awareness in emergency response, highlighting its role in reducing stress, improving decision-making, and enhancing overall performance.

Self-awareness involves understanding one's values, strengths, and weaknesses, as well as recognizing emotional triggers and patterns. By developing self-awareness, responders can better navigate complex situations, such as hostage negotiations or crowd control, where emotions can run high. Chase Hughes' Influence Code provides a framework for building self-awareness through techniques like introspection, self-reflection, and mindfulness.

Effective self-awareness enables responders to recognize the physical and emotional signs of stress, such as increased heart rate, sweating, or feelings of anxiety. By acknowledging these signs, responders can take proactive steps to manage their emotions, such as taking a few deep breaths, stepping back from the situation, or seeking support from colleagues. This helps maintain emotional control, even in the most challenging situations.

The National Crisis Institute's studies have shown that emergency responders with high self-awareness are better equipped to handle stress and make sound decisions under pressure. For example, a study on crisis negotiation found that responders who were more self-aware were more effective in de-escalating conflicts and resolving crises peacefully. By prioritizing self-awareness, responders like Ethan Slade can develop the emotional control needed to excel in high-pressure situations and provide better support to individuals and communities in need.

Chase Hughes' Influence Code emphasizes the importance of self-awareness in emergency response, providing responders with the tools and techniques necessary to build this critical skill. By developing self-awareness, responders can enhance their performance, reduce stress, and improve outcomes in even the most volatile situations.

Building on the foundation of self-awareness, emergency responders like Ethan Slade can develop emotional control by recognizing and managing their emotional triggers. The National Crisis Institute's research highlights the significance of identifying personal emotional triggers, such as frustration, anxiety, or fear, which can impact decision-making and behavior in high-pressure situations. By acknowledging these triggers, responders can develop strategies to mitigate their effects, ensuring a more measured and effective response.

For instance, a responder who recognizes that they become frustrated when dealing with uncooperative individuals can prepare themselves for such interactions by taking a few deep breaths, counting to ten, or stepping back to reassess the situation. This brief pause can help the responder regain emotional control, respond more thoughtfully, and de-escalate potential conflicts. Chase Hughes' Influence Code provides responders with practical techniques, such as emotional labeling and cognitive reappraisal, to manage their emotions and maintain control in challenging situations.

The importance of self-awareness in maintaining emotional control is further underscored by the concept of emotional contagion. In high-pressure situations, responders can "catch" emotions from those around them, such as anxiety or panic, which can compromise their ability to respond effectively. By being aware of their own emotions and those of others, responders can take steps to mitigate the spread of negative emotions and create a more positive and calm environment. This, in turn, can help to de-escalate conflicts, reduce stress, and improve outcomes.

The National Crisis Institute's training programs emphasize the value of self-awareness in emergency response, providing responders with the tools and techniques necessary to develop this critical skill. By prioritizing self-awareness and emotional control, responders like Ethan Slade can enhance their performance, reduce stress, and improve outcomes in even the most volatile situations. Chase Hughes' Influence Code offers a comprehensive framework for building self-awareness and emotional control, enabling responders to provide better support to individuals and communities in need.

Strategies for Mitigating the Effects of Chronic Stress on Performance

Chronic stress can significantly impact the performance of emergency responders like Ethan Slade. Prolonged exposure to high-pressure situations can lead to decreased focus, impaired decision-making, and reduced reaction times. The National Crisis Institute's research highlights the importance of mitigating the effects of chronic stress on performance, as it can compromise the safety and effectiveness of emergency response efforts.

One key strategy for mitigating the effects of chronic stress is prioritizing self-care. Emergency responders must recognize the importance of maintaining their physical and mental well-being, through activities such as regular exercise, healthy eating, and sufficient sleep. By taking care of their overall health, responders can improve their resilience to stress and enhance their ability to perform under pressure. Chase Hughes' Influence Code emphasizes the value of self-care in emergency response, providing responders with practical techniques for managing stress and maintaining peak performance.

Another critical strategy is developing effective coping mechanisms. Emergency responders must learn to manage their stress levels in real-time, using techniques such as deep breathing, visualization, or positive self-talk. These coping mechanisms can help responders stay focused and calm, even in the most chaotic situations. The National Crisis Institute's training programs provide responders with evidence-based coping strategies, enabling them to better manage the emotional and psychological demands of their work.

Additionally, emergency response teams must foster a supportive and collaborative environment, where responders feel comfortable sharing their concerns and receiving support from colleagues. This can help reduce feelings of isolation and burnout, which are common among emergency responders. By promoting a culture of mutual support and respect, teams can enhance their overall performance and better manage the effects of chronic stress. Chase Hughes' Influence Code provides guidance on building and maintaining high-performing teams, emphasizing the importance of trust, communication, and collaboration in emergency response.

Effective stress management is crucial for emergency responders like Ethan Slade to maintain peak performance. The National Crisis Institute's research emphasizes the importance of recognizing early warning signs of chronic stress, such as decreased motivation, increased irritability, or physical symptoms like headaches or fatigue. By acknowledging these signs, responders can take proactive steps to mitigate the effects of stress and prevent burnout.

Chase Hughes' Influence Code provides a comprehensive framework for managing stress, including techniques like emotional labeling, cognitive reappraisal, and mindfulness meditation. These strategies enable responders to better regulate their emotions, manage stress, and maintain focus in high-pressure situations. For example, a responder who recognizes they are feeling anxious or overwhelmed can use emotional labeling to acknowledge and accept their emotions, rather than trying to suppress them. This simple yet powerful technique can help reduce stress and improve performance.

Emergency response teams can also benefit from implementing stress-reducing protocols, such as regular debriefing sessions, peer support groups, or access to mental health resources. These initiatives can help responders process their experiences, share concerns, and receive support from colleagues and mental health professionals. By prioritizing stress management and providing a supportive environment, teams can enhance their overall resilience and better manage the effects of chronic stress.

Furthermore, technology can play a critical role in mitigating the effects of chronic stress on performance. Mobile apps, wearable devices, and other digital tools can help responders track their physical and mental well-being, receive personalized feedback, and access stress-reducing resources. The National Crisis Institute's research highlights the potential benefits of leveraging technology to support stress management, including improved responder safety, enhanced performance, and reduced turnover rates. By embracing innovative solutions and prioritizing stress management, emergency response teams can better navigate the challenges of high-pressure situations and maintain peak performance.

Techniques for Regulating Emotions and Staying Focused Under Pressure

Emergency responders like Ethan Slade face high-pressure situations that demand effective emotional regulation and focus. The National Crisis Institute's research emphasizes the critical role of emotional control in managing volatile situations, such as riots or hostage standoffs. Responders who can regulate their emotions and stay focused under pressure are better equipped to make sound decisions, communicate effectively, and guide individuals toward safer outcomes.

Chase Hughes' Influence Code provides a comprehensive framework for regulating emotions and maintaining focus in high-stress environments. This includes techniques like mindfulness, deep breathing, and cognitive reappraisal, which enable responders to manage stress, anxiety, and other emotions that can impede performance. By mastering these techniques, responders can improve their ability to stay focused, think critically, and make effective decisions in the face of uncertainty.

Effective emotional regulation is also closely tied to trust-building and strategic communication. When responders can manage their emotions and communicate clearly, they are more likely to establish trust with individuals or crowds, which is critical for de-escalating tense situations and promoting safer outcomes. The National Crisis Institute's research highlights the importance of empathy and active listening in building trust and resolving conflicts, and responders who can regulate their emotions are better positioned to employ these skills effectively.

Furthermore, emotional regulation and focus are essential for maintaining situational awareness, which is critical for emergency responders. By staying focused and aware of their surroundings, responders can quickly assess situations, identify potential threats, and respond effectively to changing circumstances. This requires a high degree of emotional control, as well as the ability to prioritize tasks, manage distractions, and maintain a clear sense of purpose. By developing these skills, responders like Ethan Slade can improve their performance, enhance public safety, and save lives in critical moments.

The ability to regulate emotions and stay focused under pressure is crucial for emergency responders like Ethan Slade. Chase Hughes' Influence Code provides responders with techniques to manage stress and maintain emotional control, even in the most volatile situations. For example, the "emotional labeling" technique involves acknowledging and accepting emotions, rather than trying to suppress them. This simple yet effective strategy can help responders reduce stress and improve their ability to think critically.

Responders who master emotional regulation can also improve their communication skills, which is critical for building trust and resolving conflicts. By managing their emotions, responders can communicate more clearly and empathetically, which helps to de-escalate tense situations and promote safer outcomes. The National Crisis Institute's research highlights the importance of active listening and empathy in crisis negotiation, and responders who can regulate their emotions are better equipped to employ these skills effectively.

In addition to emotional regulation, maintaining focus under pressure is critical for emergency responders. This requires a high degree of situational awareness, as well as the ability to prioritize tasks and manage distractions. Responders who can maintain focus can quickly assess situations, identify potential threats, and respond effectively to changing circumstances. The National Crisis Institute's training programs emphasize the importance of maintaining focus under pressure, and provide responders with techniques to improve their situational awareness and decision-making skills.

The use of mindfulness and deep breathing exercises can also help responders manage stress and maintain emotional control. These techniques can be used in high-pressure situations to reduce anxiety and improve focus. For example, a responder who is negotiating with a hostage-taker can use deep breathing exercises to calm their nerves and maintain a clear head. This helps the responder to think critically and make effective decisions, even in the most intense and dynamic situations.

By mastering the techniques outlined in Chase Hughes' Influence Code, emergency responders like Ethan Slade can improve their ability to regulate emotions and stay focused under pressure. This enables them to perform more effectively in high-stress environments, build trust with individuals and crowds, and promote safer outcomes in critical situations.

Chapter 8: "Advanced Influence Tactics for Complex Emergency Response Situations"

Establishing Trust and Credibility in High-Pressure Environments

Establishing trust and credibility is crucial for emergency responders like Ethan Slade, who often find themselves in high-pressure situations where lives are at stake. The National Crisis Institute's research emphasizes the significance of trust-building in crisis management, highlighting its impact on de-escalating volatile situations and promoting safer outcomes. Trust is built when responders demonstrate empathy, active listening, and a genuine understanding of the individual's or crowd's concerns.

In high-pressure environments, responders must establish trust quickly, often within minutes or even seconds. This requires a deep understanding of human behavior, emotional intelligence, and effective communication strategies. Chase Hughes' Influence Code provides responders with the tools to build trust rapidly, leveraging techniques such as mirroring, open-ended questioning, and emotional labeling. These tactics enable responders to create a connection with individuals or crowds, fostering an environment of mutual understanding and cooperation.

Effective trust-building also relies on credibility, which is established when responders demonstrate expertise, confidence, and a calm demeanor. Responders who exude confidence and composure are more likely to be perceived as trustworthy and credible, even in the most chaotic situations. The National Crisis Institute's training programs focus on developing these skills, providing responders with the knowledge and techniques necessary to project confidence and credibility in high-pressure environments.

Real-world examples illustrate the importance of trust and credibility in emergency response situations. For instance, during a hostage standoff, a responder who establishes trust with the hostage-taker can create an opportunity for negotiation, increasing the chances of a peaceful resolution. Similarly, in a riot situation, responders who build trust with crowd leaders can influence the crowd's behavior, reducing the risk of violence and promoting a safer outcome. By mastering the art of trust-building and credibility establishment, emergency responders like Ethan Slade can enhance their ability to manage complex emergency response situations, ultimately saving lives and reducing harm.

Building on the foundation of trust and credibility, emergency responders must also demonstrate empathy and understanding in high-pressure situations. This involves actively listening to individuals or crowds, acknowledging their concerns, and validating their emotions. Chase Hughes' Influence Code emphasizes the importance of emotional intelligence in crisis management, providing responders with techniques to recognize and manage their own emotions, as well as those of others.

In a mass casualty incident, for example, responders who demonstrate empathy and compassion can help alleviate panic and anxiety, creating an environment more conducive to effective emergency response. By acknowledging the emotional toll of the situation on those affected, responders can establish a connection with the crowd, fostering cooperation and reducing the risk of chaos. The National Crisis Institute's research highlights the significance of empathy in crisis management, demonstrating its impact on de-escalating volatile situations and promoting safer outcomes.

Responders must also be aware of their nonverbal communication, as body language and tone of voice can significantly influence trust and credibility. Maintaining a calm and composed demeanor, even in the most chaotic situations, is crucial for projecting confidence and control. The use of open and approachable body language, such as uncrossing arms or standing with an open posture, can help create a sense of rapport with individuals or crowds, facilitating more effective communication.

Real-world examples illustrate the effectiveness of these tactics in high-pressure environments. During a natural disaster response, responders who establish trust and credibility with affected communities can facilitate more efficient evacuation procedures, reducing the risk of harm to both responders and civilians. Similarly, in a hostage negotiation scenario, responders who demonstrate empathy and understanding can create an opportunity for dialogue, increasing the chances of a peaceful resolution. By mastering the art of establishing trust and credibility, emergency responders like Ethan Slade can enhance their ability to manage complex emergency response situations, ultimately saving lives and reducing harm.

The National Crisis Institute's training programs provide responders with hands-on experience in applying these tactics, simulating real-world scenarios to develop the skills necessary for effective trust-building and crisis management. By combining theoretical knowledge with practical application, responders can develop the expertise required to establish trust and credibility in high-pressure environments, ensuring a more effective response to complex emergency situations.

Leveraging Emotional Intelligence to De-Escalate Volatile Situations

Leveraging Emotional Intelligence to De-Escalate Volatile Situations

Emergency responders like Ethan Slade face high-stress situations where emotions run high, and panic can quickly escalate into chaos. In these critical moments, emotional intelligence plays a crucial role in de-escalating volatile situations. The National Crisis Institute's research emphasizes the significance of emotional intelligence in crisis management, highlighting its impact on reducing conflict and promoting safer outcomes.

Emotional intelligence involves recognizing and managing one's own emotions, as well as those of others. In emergency response situations, this means being aware of the emotional tone of a crowd or individual and adapting communication strategies to address their concerns. Chase Hughes' Influence Code provides responders with techniques to develop emotional intelligence, including self-awareness, empathy, and social skills.

In a riot situation, for example, responders who demonstrate empathy and understanding can help calm the crowd, reducing the risk of violence and promoting a safer environment. By acknowledging the emotional toll of the situation on individuals, responders can establish a connection with the crowd, fostering cooperation and de-escalating tensions. The National Crisis Institute's training programs focus on developing these skills, providing responders with hands-on experience in managing emotions and de-escalating conflicts.

Effective communication is also critical in de-escalating volatile situations. Responders must be able to articulate their message clearly, avoiding triggers that may escalate the situation. Active listening is essential, as it allows responders to understand the concerns and needs of individuals or crowds, addressing them in a timely and effective manner. The Influence Code provides responders with strategies for effective communication, including verbal and nonverbal cues, to facilitate de-escalation and promote safer outcomes.

Real-world examples illustrate the effectiveness of emotional intelligence in emergency response situations. During a hostage standoff, responders who demonstrate empathy and understanding can create an opportunity for dialogue, increasing the chances of a peaceful resolution. Similarly, in a mass evacuation scenario, responders who manage emotions effectively can reduce panic and anxiety, facilitating a more efficient and safer evacuation process. By mastering the art of emotional intelligence, emergency responders like Ethan Slade can enhance their ability to de-escalate volatile situations, ultimately saving lives and reducing harm.

Emotional intelligence is crucial in de-escalating volatile situations, and its application can be observed in various emergency response scenarios. For instance, during a mass protest, responders who employ emotional intelligence can identify potential flashpoints and intervene early to prevent escalation. By recognizing the emotional tone of the crowd and adapting their communication strategy, responders can reduce tensions and promote a peaceful resolution.

The National Crisis Institute's research highlights the significance of empathy in de-escalating conflicts. Responders who demonstrate empathy can establish trust with individuals or crowds, creating an environment conducive to dialogue and cooperation. This is particularly important in situations where emotions are running high, and parties may be resistant to reasoning. By acknowledging the emotional concerns of all parties involved, responders can facilitate a more constructive conversation, leading to a safer and more effective resolution.

Effective communication is also critical in leveraging emotional intelligence. Responders must be able to articulate their message clearly, avoiding triggers that may escalate the situation. Active listening is essential, as it allows responders to understand the concerns and needs of individuals or crowds, addressing them in a timely and effective manner. The Influence Code provides responders with strategies for effective communication, including verbal and nonverbal cues, to facilitate de-escalation and promote safer outcomes.

A key aspect of emotional intelligence is self-awareness, which enables responders to recognize and manage their own emotions. This is critical in high-stress situations, where responders may be exposed to traumatic or disturbing events. By being aware of their own emotional state, responders can maintain a level head, making more effective decisions and responding more appropriately to the situation. The National Crisis Institute's training programs emphasize the importance of self-awareness, providing responders with techniques to manage their emotions and maintain a professional demeanor, even in the most challenging situations.

Real-world examples demonstrate the effectiveness of emotional intelligence in emergency response situations. During a hostage standoff, responders who employed emotional intelligence were able to establish a rapport with the hostage-taker, creating an opportunity for dialogue and ultimately securing the safe release of the hostages. Similarly, in a mass evacuation scenario, responders who managed emotions effectively were able to reduce panic and anxiety, facilitating a more efficient and safer evacuation process. By mastering the art of emotional intelligence, emergency responders like Ethan Slade can enhance their ability to de-escalate volatile situations, ultimately saving lives and reducing harm.

Strategic Communication Techniques for Crisis Negotiation

Strategic communication techniques are vital in crisis negotiation, where the stakes are high and every word counts. Emergency responders like Ethan Slade must be equipped with the skills to navigate complex situations, build trust, and guide individuals or crowds toward safer decisions. The National Crisis Institute's research emphasizes the significance of strategic communication in de-escalating conflicts and promoting positive outcomes.

Effective crisis negotiation relies on a deep understanding of human behavior, emotional intelligence, and advanced communication techniques. Responders must be able to read people, recognize emotional cues, and adapt their approach accordingly. This requires a high degree of self-awareness, empathy, and social skills, all of which are essential components of Chase Hughes' Influence Code.

In a hostage standoff, for example, strategic communication can mean the difference between a peaceful resolution and a tragic outcome. Responders who employ active listening skills, ask open-ended questions, and acknowledge the emotions of all parties involved can create an environment conducive to dialogue and cooperation. By building trust and establishing a rapport with the hostage-taker, responders can increase the chances of a successful negotiation and minimize the risk of harm to all individuals involved.

The Influence Code provides responders with a framework for strategic communication, including techniques such as mirroring, labeling, and emotional labeling. These strategies enable responders to build connections with individuals, manage emotions, and guide conversations toward positive outcomes. By mastering these techniques, emergency responders can enhance their ability to navigate complex crisis situations, reduce conflict, and promote safer decisions.

Real-world examples demonstrate the effectiveness of strategic communication in crisis negotiation. During a mass evacuation, responders who employed advanced communication techniques were able to calm panicked individuals, provide clear instructions, and facilitate a more efficient and safer evacuation process. In a riot situation, responders who used strategic communication to build trust and establish a rapport with crowd leaders were able to de-escalate tensions and prevent further violence. By applying the principles of strategic communication, emergency responders can make a significant difference in the outcome of critical incidents, saving lives and reducing harm.

Strategic communication techniques in crisis negotiation require a nuanced understanding of human psychology and behavior. Responders must be able to recognize and respond to emotional cues, using techniques such as emotional labeling to acknowledge and validate the emotions of all parties involved. This can help to create a sense of trust and rapport, increasing the likelihood of a successful negotiation.

The National Crisis Institute's research highlights the importance of active listening in crisis negotiation. Responders who use active listening skills, such as paraphrasing and reflecting, can build trust and establish a connection with individuals, even in high-stress situations. By repeating back what they have heard and asking open-ended questions, responders can ensure that they understand the individual's concerns and needs, and respond accordingly.

In a crisis situation, time is of the essence. Responders must be able to think on their feet, using advanced communication techniques to de-escalate tensions and guide conversations toward positive outcomes. The Influence Code provides responders with a framework for strategic communication, including techniques such as mirroring and anchoring. These strategies enable responders to build connections with individuals, manage emotions, and guide conversations toward safer decisions.

A critical aspect of strategic communication in crisis negotiation is the use of language. Responders must be able to use language that is clear, concise, and non-threatening, avoiding phrases or words that may escalate the situation. By using "what" and "how" questions, responders can encourage individuals to think critically and come up with their own solutions, rather than simply reacting to a situation.

Real-world examples demonstrate the effectiveness of strategic communication in crisis negotiation. During a hostage standoff, responders who used emotional labeling and active listening skills were able to build trust with the hostage-taker, ultimately securing the release of the hostages without incident. In a riot situation, responders who employed advanced communication techniques, such as mirroring and anchoring, were able to de-escalate tensions and prevent further violence. By applying the principles of strategic communication, emergency responders can make a significant difference in the outcome of critical incidents, saving lives and reducing harm.

The Influence Code's approach to strategic communication in crisis negotiation emphasizes the importance of flexibility and adaptability. Responders must be able to adjust their approach as needed, responding to changing circumstances and evolving situations. By combining advanced communication techniques with a deep understanding of human psychology and behavior, responders can navigate even the most complex crisis situations, guiding conversations toward positive outcomes and safer decisions.

Influence Strategies for Managing Crowd Dynamics and Behavior

Managing crowd dynamics and behavior is a critical aspect of emergency response, requiring a deep understanding of human psychology and behavior. Ethan Slade, as an emergency responder, must be equipped with the skills to navigate complex situations, build trust, and guide crowds toward safer decisions. The National Crisis Institute's research emphasizes the significance of influence strategies in defusing panic and confusion, highlighting the need for responders to master the art of trust-building, empathic listening, and strategic communication.

Influence strategies play a crucial role in shaping crowd behavior, particularly in high-stress situations such as riots or mass evacuations. By employing techniques such as emotional labeling, responders can acknowledge and validate the emotions of individuals within the crowd, reducing tension and creating an environment conducive to cooperation. This approach enables responders to build trust and establish a rapport with crowd leaders, increasing the likelihood of a peaceful resolution.

The Influence Code provides a framework for managing crowd dynamics, focusing on the development of advanced communication skills and emotional intelligence. Responders who can read people, recognize emotional cues, and adapt their approach accordingly are better equipped to navigate complex situations and guide crowds toward safer decisions. Chase Hughes' proven methods, refined at the National Crisis Institute, demonstrate the effectiveness of influence strategies in real-world scenarios, from de-escalating violent confrontations to facilitating orderly evacuations.

Effective crowd management requires a nuanced understanding of group dynamics and behavior. Responders must be able to identify and respond to emotional contagion, where the emotions of one individual can spread rapidly throughout the crowd. By using techniques such as mirroring and anchoring, responders can create a sense of calm and stability, reducing the likelihood of panic and chaos. The Influence Code's approach to crowd management emphasizes the importance of flexibility and adaptability, enabling responders to adjust their strategy as needed in response to changing circumstances.

Real-world examples illustrate the power of influence strategies in managing crowd dynamics. During a recent riot, responders who employed emotional labeling and empathic listening skills were able to de-escalate tensions and prevent further violence. In a mass evacuation scenario, responders who used strategic communication and trust-building techniques were able to facilitate an orderly exit, minimizing the risk of panic and injury. By mastering the art of influence, emergency responders like Ethan Slade can make a significant difference in the outcome of critical incidents, saving lives and reducing harm.

The art of managing crowd dynamics requires a profound understanding of the psychological and social factors that drive human behavior in group settings. By recognizing the key influences that shape crowd behavior, responders can develop targeted strategies to mitigate potential threats and promote safer outcomes. Emotional contagion, for instance, plays a significant role in crowd dynamics, where the emotions of one individual can rapidly spread throughout the group. Responders who can identify and address emotional contagion early on can prevent the escalation of violent or destructive behavior.

Chase Hughes' Influence Code provides a comprehensive framework for managing crowd dynamics, emphasizing the importance of empathy, active listening, and strategic communication. By employing techniques such as mirroring and anchoring, responders can create a sense of connection with crowd leaders and influencers, increasing the likelihood of cooperation and reducing the risk of conflict. The code also highlights the significance of cultural and social awareness, recognizing that crowd behavior can be heavily influenced by cultural norms, values, and beliefs.

Real-world examples illustrate the effectiveness of influence strategies in managing crowd dynamics. During a recent protest, responders who used empathic listening skills and acknowledged the concerns of protesters were able to de-escalate tensions and prevent violence. In a mass gathering scenario, responders who employed strategic communication and trust-building techniques were able to facilitate a safe and orderly evacuation, despite the presence of multiple potential hazards.

The National Crisis Institute's research has also identified the importance of crowd mapping, a technique used to identify and analyze the social dynamics within a crowd. By recognizing key individuals and groups, responders can develop targeted strategies to influence behavior and promote safer outcomes. Crowd mapping involves identifying crowd leaders, influencers, and other key players, as well as recognizing patterns of behavior and communication within the group.

In addition to crowd mapping, responders must also be aware of the physical environment and its impact on crowd behavior. Environmental factors such as noise levels, temperature, and visibility can all contribute to increased tension and anxiety within a crowd. By recognizing these factors and taking steps to mitigate their effects, responders can reduce the risk of conflict and promote a safer environment.

The Influence Code's approach to managing crowd dynamics is centered on the development of advanced communication skills and emotional intelligence. Responders who can read people, recognize emotional cues, and adapt their approach accordingly are better equipped to navigate complex situations and guide crowds toward safer outcomes. By mastering the art of influence, emergency responders can make a significant difference in the outcome of critical incidents, saving lives and reducing harm. Ultimately, the effective management of crowd dynamics requires a deep understanding of human behavior, a nuanced awareness of social and cultural factors, and a commitment to empathy, active listening, and strategic communication.

Tactical Empathy and Active Listening in Emergency Response

Tactical empathy and active listening are critical components of effective emergency response, enabling responders to build trust and guide individuals or crowds toward safer decisions. Chase Hughes' Influence Code emphasizes the importance of these skills in high-pressure situations, where every moment counts. By employing tactical empathy and active listening, responders can defuse tension, reduce anxiety, and create an environment conducive to cooperation.

In emergency response situations, such as hostage standoffs or riots, the ability to establish a rapport with individuals or crowd leaders is crucial. Tactical empathy allows responders to understand the perspectives, needs, and concerns of those involved, enabling them to develop targeted strategies that address the root causes of the situation. Active listening is equally essential, as it enables responders to gather vital information, recognize emotional cues, and respond in a way that acknowledges and validates the emotions of others.

The National Crisis Institute's research has demonstrated the effectiveness of tactical empathy and active listening in emergency response situations. By using open-ended questions, reflective listening, and emotional labeling, responders can create a sense of safety and trust, reducing the likelihood of escalation and promoting a peaceful resolution. For example, in a hostage situation, a responder who uses tactical empathy to understand the motivations and concerns of the hostage-taker may be able to establish a rapport and negotiate a safe release.

Tactical empathy is not about agreeing with or sympathizing with the individual's actions, but rather about understanding their perspective and using that understanding to inform response strategies. Active listening is a key component of this process, as it enables responders to gather information, recognize patterns of behavior, and respond in a way that addresses the underlying needs and concerns. By combining tactical empathy with active listening, responders can create a powerful toolkit for managing volatile situations and guiding individuals or crowds toward safer outcomes.

In emergency response situations, every interaction counts, and the ability to establish trust and rapport is critical. Tactical empathy and active listening are essential skills for any responder, as they enable them to navigate complex situations, reduce tension, and promote cooperation. By mastering these skills, responders can make a significant difference in the outcome of critical incidents, saving lives and reducing harm. The Influence Code's approach to tactical empathy and active listening provides a comprehensive framework for emergency responders to develop these essential skills and apply them in high-pressure situations.

Effective tactical empathy and active listening require a deep understanding of human behavior, emotional intelligence, and advanced communication skills. Responders must be able to recognize and interpret nonverbal cues, such as body language and tone of voice, to accurately assess the situation and respond accordingly. This skillset is particularly critical in high-stress environments, where emotions can run high and decision-making is impaired.

The Influence Code's approach to tactical empathy emphasizes the importance of mirroring and anchoring techniques. Mirroring involves reflecting the emotional state and language patterns of the individual or crowd, creating a sense of connection and rapport. Anchoring, on the other hand, involves identifying and leveraging key influencers or leaders within the group to shape behavior and promote cooperation. By combining these techniques, responders can establish trust and credibility, reducing the likelihood of conflict and promoting a peaceful resolution.

A notable example of the effectiveness of tactical empathy and active listening can be seen in a recent mass evacuation scenario. Responders used open-ended questions and reflective listening to understand the concerns and needs of evacuees, addressing fears and anxieties in real-time. By doing so, they created a sense of safety and trust, facilitating a smooth and orderly evacuation despite the presence of multiple hazards. This approach not only saved lives but also reduced the risk of secondary incidents and injuries.

The National Crisis Institute's research has also highlighted the importance of cultural competence in tactical empathy and active listening. Responders must be aware of cultural nuances and differences to effectively communicate and build trust with diverse populations. This requires a deep understanding of cultural norms, values, and communication patterns, as well as the ability to adapt response strategies accordingly.

Tactical empathy and active listening are not limited to verbal communication; they also involve nonverbal cues and environmental factors. Responders must be aware of their own body language and tone of voice, ensuring that they convey a sense of calm and professionalism in high-stress situations. Additionally, the physical environment can play a significant role in shaping behavior and promoting cooperation. For example, responders may use spatial arrangements and visual cues to create a sense of safety and order, reducing anxiety and promoting a peaceful resolution.

The Influence Code's approach to tactical empathy and active listening provides a comprehensive framework for emergency responders to develop these essential skills and apply them in complex emergency response situations. By combining advanced communication techniques with a deep understanding of human behavior and emotional intelligence, responders can create a powerful toolkit for managing volatile situations, reducing conflict, and promoting cooperation. This skillset is critical in today's fast-paced and increasingly complex emergency response environment, where the ability to establish trust and rapport can mean the difference between life and death.

Advanced Psychological Tactics for Resolving Complex Conflicts

Advanced psychological tactics play a crucial role in resolving complex conflicts that arise during emergency response situations. These tactics enable responders to navigate volatile environments, build trust with individuals or crowds, and guide them toward safer decisions. Chase Hughes' Influence Code provides a comprehensive framework for mastering these advanced psychological tactics, which are rooted in proven methods refined at the National Crisis Institute.

Effective conflict resolution in emergency response situations requires a deep understanding of human behavior, emotional intelligence, and strategic communication. Responders must be able to recognize and interpret behavioral cues, such as body language and speech patterns, to assess the situation accurately and respond accordingly. This skillset is critical in high-stress environments, where emotions can run high and decision-making is impaired.

The Influence Code's approach to advanced psychological tactics emphasizes the importance of trust-building and empathic listening. By establishing a rapport with individuals or crowds, responders can create a sense of safety and security, reducing anxiety and promoting cooperation. This is particularly critical in situations where fear, anger, or confusion may be driving behavior. For example, during a hostage standoff, responders who use empathic listening to understand the motivations and concerns of the hostage-taker may be able to establish a connection and negotiate a peaceful resolution.

Strategic communication is another key component of advanced psychological tactics. Responders must be able to craft messages that resonate with their audience, taking into account cultural nuances, emotional state, and cognitive biases. This requires a deep understanding of human psychology and behavior, as well as the ability to adapt communication strategies in real-time. The National Crisis Institute's research has shown that responders who use strategic communication techniques, such as mirroring and reframing, can significantly reduce conflict escalation and promote more positive outcomes.

The application of advanced psychological tactics in emergency response situations is not limited to verbal communication; nonverbal cues and environmental factors also play a significant role. Responders must be aware of their own body language and tone of voice, ensuring that they convey a sense of calm and professionalism in high-stress situations. Additionally, the physical environment can be used to create a sense of safety and order, reducing anxiety and promoting cooperation. For instance, responders may use spatial arrangements and visual cues to guide individuals or crowds toward safer areas, reducing the risk of secondary incidents.

By mastering advanced psychological tactics, emergency responders can develop the skills necessary to resolve complex conflicts effectively. The Influence Code provides a comprehensive framework for achieving this goal, offering evidence-based strategies and techniques that have been proven to work in real-world emergency response situations. Whether responding to riots, hostage standoffs, or mass evacuations, responders who employ these advanced psychological tactics can save lives, reduce conflict, and promote more positive outcomes.

The Influence Code's framework for advanced psychological tactics emphasizes the critical role of emotional intelligence in conflict resolution. Responders who can accurately assess and manage their own emotions are better equipped to navigate high-stress situations and make effective decisions. This self-awareness also enables responders to recognize and respond to the emotional cues of others, building trust and rapport with individuals or crowds.

A key tactic in the Influence Code is the use of "emotional labeling," which involves acknowledging and validating the emotions of others. By doing so, responders can create a sense of safety and understanding, reducing anxiety and promoting cooperation. For example, during a mass evacuation, a responder who acknowledges the fear and uncertainty of evacuees can help to calm them and facilitate a more orderly exit.

The National Crisis Institute's research has also highlighted the importance of cognitive biases in conflict resolution. Responders must be aware of their own biases and those of others, taking steps to mitigate their impact on decision-making. This includes recognizing the role of confirmation bias, where individuals tend to favor information that confirms their existing beliefs, and anchoring bias, where initial information influences subsequent decisions.

To counter these biases, responders can use techniques such as "perspective-taking," which involves considering alternative viewpoints and challenging assumptions. This can help to reduce conflict escalation and promote more effective communication. For instance, during a hostage negotiation, a responder who takes the perspective of the hostage-taker may be able to identify underlying motivations and concerns, developing a more targeted and effective response.

The Influence Code also emphasizes the importance of adaptability in conflict resolution. Responders must be able to adjust their tactics in real-time, responding to changing circumstances and evolving situations. This requires a deep understanding of human behavior and psychology, as well as the ability to think critically and make effective decisions under pressure.

A critical aspect of adaptability is the use of "feedback loops," which involve continuously assessing and adjusting responses based on feedback from others. By doing so, responders can refine their tactics and improve outcomes, reducing conflict escalation and promoting more positive results. For example, during a riot, responders who use feedback loops to assess the impact of their tactics can adjust their approach to better address the needs and concerns of the crowd, reducing violence and promoting a more peaceful resolution.

By mastering these advanced psychological tactics, emergency responders can develop the skills necessary to resolve complex conflicts effectively. The Influence Code provides a comprehensive framework for achieving this goal, offering evidence-based strategies and techniques that have been proven to work in real-world emergency response situations. Whether responding to riots, hostage standoffs, or mass evacuations, responders who employ these advanced psychological tactics can save lives, reduce conflict, and promote more positive outcomes.

Chapter 9: "Ethical Considerations and Boundaries in Emergency Response Persuasion"

Respecting Autonomy in High-Pressure Situations

Respecting autonomy in high-pressure situations is crucial for emergency responders. During critical moments like riots or hostage standoffs, individuals may feel overwhelmed, leading to impaired decision-making. Effective persuasion strategies must balance the need to guide people toward safer choices with respect for their autonomy.

Emergency responders face a delicate challenge: they must protect people while also acknowledging their right to make decisions. Hughes' influence methods, refined at the National Crisis Institute, prioritize building trust and establishing rapport with individuals or crowds. This approach recognizes that people are more likely to accept guidance when they feel understood and respected.

In high-stress situations, autonomy can be compromised by factors like fear, anxiety, or confusion. Emergency responders must be aware of these dynamics and adapt their persuasion strategies accordingly. By doing so, they can empower individuals to make informed decisions that align with their own values and interests.

The National Crisis Institute's research highlights the importance of preserving autonomy in emergency response situations. Studies have shown that when people feel their autonomy is respected, they are more likely to cooperate with responders and follow instructions. This cooperation can be critical in preventing harm and resolving crises efficiently.

Emergency responders must also consider the potential consequences of compromising autonomy. Coercive or manipulative tactics can damage trust and lead to negative outcomes, including increased resistance or even violence. In contrast, respectful and empathetic approaches can foster a sense of collaboration, reducing the risk of conflict and promoting more effective crisis resolution.

By prioritizing autonomy and using evidence-based persuasion strategies, emergency responders can navigate complex situations while maintaining the trust and cooperation of those involved. This approach is essential for saving lives and minimizing harm in critical moments, and it forms the foundation of Hughes' Influence Code.

Emergency responders must strike a balance between guiding individuals toward safer choices and respecting their autonomy. This balance is particularly challenging in situations where people's lives are at risk, such as hostage standoffs or mass evacuations. Hughes' influence methods emphasize the importance of empathetic listening and strategic communication in building trust and establishing rapport with those involved.

During high-pressure situations, responders must be aware of the power dynamics at play. Individuals in crisis may feel vulnerable, disempowered, or traumatized, which can compromise their ability to make informed decisions. Responders who prioritize autonomy recognize these dynamics and adapt their approach to empower individuals, rather than exploiting their vulnerability.

The National Crisis Institute's research highlights the significance of cultural sensitivity in respecting autonomy. Emergency responders must consider the diverse backgrounds, values, and beliefs of those they interact with, tailoring their persuasion strategies to accommodate these differences. For example, in a hostage situation involving a culturally or linguistically diverse group, responders who take the time to understand and respect these differences can build trust more effectively, increasing the likelihood of a peaceful resolution.

Effective persuasion strategies also involve transparency and honesty. Responders must clearly communicate their intentions, motivations, and goals, avoiding manipulative or coercive tactics that can erode trust. By being transparent, responders demonstrate respect for individuals' autonomy, acknowledging their right to make informed decisions about their own lives.

A notable example of respecting autonomy in emergency response is the use of crisis negotiation teams. These teams prioritize building rapport and establishing trust with individuals in crisis, rather than relying on aggressive or confrontational tactics. By doing so, they create a safe space for open communication, empowering individuals to express their concerns and needs. This approach has proven effective in resolving high-pressure situations, such as hostage standoffs, without resorting to force.

The consequences of disregarding autonomy can be severe. Coercive or manipulative tactics can lead to long-term psychological trauma, damage relationships between responders and the community, and compromise the effectiveness of emergency response efforts. In contrast, prioritizing autonomy fosters a culture of trust, respect, and cooperation, ultimately saving lives and minimizing harm in critical moments.

By integrating respect for autonomy into their persuasion strategies, emergency responders can navigate complex situations with greater ease, building trust and cooperation while protecting those involved. This approach is a cornerstone of Hughes' Influence Code, emphasizing the importance of empathy, transparency, and cultural sensitivity in effective crisis resolution.

Navigating Cultural and Social Biases in Persuasion

Navigating cultural and social biases is crucial for emergency responders who aim to persuade individuals or crowds in critical situations. Hughes' influence methods, refined at the National Crisis Institute, emphasize the importance of understanding and respecting these differences to build trust and establish effective communication.

Cultural biases can significantly impact persuasion efforts. Responders who fail to consider the cultural background of those they interact with may inadvertently use language, tone, or body language that is perceived as insensitive or even hostile. For instance, in a hostage situation involving individuals from a culturally diverse group, responders who are aware of the cultural nuances can adapt their communication strategy to address the specific needs and concerns of each individual.

Social biases also play a significant role in persuasion. Emergency responders may unintentionally bring their own biases to the interaction, influencing their perception of the situation and the individuals involved. Recognizing and managing these biases is essential to ensure that responders approach each situation with empathy and an open mind. The National Crisis Institute's research highlights the importance of self-awareness and cultural competence in emergency response persuasion, demonstrating that responders who are aware of their own biases are better equipped to navigate complex social dynamics.

Effective persuasion strategies must take into account the power of implicit biases. Responders who are unaware of their own biases may inadvertently perpetuate stereotypes or make assumptions about individuals based on their appearance, accent, or background. Hughes' influence methods emphasize the need for responders to engage in active self-reflection, recognizing and challenging their own biases to ensure that their communication is respectful, empathetic, and effective.

The consequences of neglecting cultural and social biases can be severe. Persuasion efforts that fail to account for these differences may be met with resistance, hostility, or even violence. In contrast, responders who prioritize cultural sensitivity and self-awareness can build trust, establish rapport, and guide individuals toward safer decisions, ultimately saving lives and minimizing harm in critical moments.

Real-world examples demonstrate the significance of navigating cultural and social biases in emergency response persuasion. For instance, during a mass evacuation, responders who are aware of the cultural and linguistic diversity of the crowd can adapt their communication strategy to ensure that everyone receives clear instructions and support. By doing so, they can reduce panic and confusion, facilitating a more efficient and safe evacuation process.

By acknowledging and addressing cultural and social biases, emergency responders can develop more effective persuasion strategies, ultimately enhancing their ability to manage critical situations and save lives. Hughes' influence methods provide a framework for responders to navigate these complex dynamics, emphasizing the importance of empathy, self-awareness, and cultural competence in building trust and guiding individuals toward safer decisions.

Hughes' influence methods emphasize the need for emergency responders to develop cultural competence, which involves understanding and respecting the values, beliefs, and practices of diverse groups. This competence is critical in high-pressure situations, where responders must make quick decisions that can have a significant impact on individuals and communities. By being aware of cultural differences, responders can adapt their communication strategy to avoid unintended offense or misinterpretation.

For example, in a crisis situation involving a family from a traditional or conservative background, responders who are sensitive to cultural norms around authority and decision-making can adjust their approach to engage with the family's patriarch or matriarch, rather than directly addressing younger family members. This nuanced understanding of cultural dynamics can help build trust and facilitate more effective communication.

Social biases also play a significant role in shaping persuasion efforts. Emergency responders may hold implicit biases that influence their perceptions of individuals or groups, often unconsciously. These biases can affect the way responders communicate, make decisions, and allocate resources. Hughes' influence methods stress the importance of recognizing and managing these biases to ensure that responders approach each situation with empathy and an open mind.

The National Crisis Institute's research highlights the value of scenario-based training in developing cultural competence and mitigating social biases. By simulating real-world crisis scenarios, responders can practice navigating complex cultural dynamics and develop the skills needed to communicate effectively with diverse groups. This training also helps responders recognize and challenge their own biases, leading to more nuanced and empathetic decision-making.

Effective persuasion strategies must also take into account the role of power dynamics in crisis situations. Emergency responders often hold a position of authority, which can impact the way individuals respond to their communication efforts. Hughes' influence methods emphasize the need for responders to be aware of these power dynamics and adapt their approach to empower individuals and communities, rather than simply imposing their will.

For instance, during a natural disaster response, responders who prioritize community engagement and participation can build trust and facilitate more effective collaboration. By working with local leaders and community members to develop response strategies, responders can ensure that their efforts are culturally sensitive and responsive to the unique needs of the affected community.

Real-world examples demonstrate the significance of navigating cultural and social biases in emergency response persuasion. The aftermath of Hurricane Katrina, for example, highlighted the importance of cultural competence in disaster response. Responders who were aware of the cultural nuances of the affected communities were better equipped to provide support and facilitate recovery efforts, while those who failed to account for these differences often exacerbated existing social and economic disparities.

By acknowledging and addressing cultural and social biases, emergency responders can develop more effective persuasion strategies that prioritize empathy, trust, and community engagement. Hughes' influence methods provide a framework for responders to navigate complex cultural dynamics, recognize and manage their own biases, and adapt their approach to the unique needs of each situation. By doing so, responders can enhance their ability to manage critical situations, save lives, and promote more equitable and just outcomes.

The Role of Deception and Misdirection in Emergency Response

The Role of Deception and Misdirection in Emergency Response

Emergency responders often face situations where the truth is not enough to persuade individuals or crowds to make safer decisions. In such cases, deception and misdirection can be valuable tools in the persuasion toolkit. Hughes' influence methods, developed at the National Crisis Institute, acknowledge the potential benefits of strategic deception in emergency response scenarios.

Deception can take many forms, from withholding information to actively providing false information. In emergency response situations, responders may use deception to prevent panic, protect sensitive information, or facilitate a safer outcome. For example, during a hostage situation, responders might deliberately release misleading information about their negotiation strategy to prevent the perpetrator from anticipating their next move.

Misdirection is another technique used to influence behavior in emergency response scenarios. By diverting attention away from the true nature of the situation, responders can create an opportunity for a safer resolution. During a mass evacuation, for instance, responders might use misdirection to redirect crowd flow away from hazardous areas, reducing the risk of injury or harm.

The key to effective deception and misdirection in emergency response is to ensure that these tactics are used ethically and with careful consideration of their potential consequences. Responders must weigh the benefits of deception against the risks of discovery and the potential erosion of trust. Hughes' influence methods emphasize the importance of transparency and honesty in building trust with individuals and crowds, but also acknowledge that there may be situations where strategic deception is necessary to achieve a safer outcome.

The National Crisis Institute's research highlights the need for responders to carefully consider the context and motivations behind their use of deception and misdirection. In some cases, deception may be used to exploit vulnerabilities or manipulate individuals, which can have negative consequences and undermine trust in the long term. Responders must be aware of these risks and take steps to mitigate them, ensuring that their use of deception and misdirection is proportionate to the situation and respectful of the individuals involved.

Real-world examples demonstrate the effectiveness of deception and misdirection in emergency response scenarios. During the 1993 World Trade Center bombing, responders used misdirection to evacuate people from the building while minimizing panic and chaos. By providing clear and direct instructions, while also withholding sensitive information about the extent of the damage, responders were able to facilitate a safer evacuation and reduce the risk of injury or harm.

Hughes' influence methods provide a framework for emergency responders to navigate the complex ethical considerations surrounding deception and misdirection in emergency response scenarios. By understanding the potential benefits and risks of these tactics, responders can develop the skills needed to use them effectively and responsibly, ultimately saving lives and promoting safer outcomes in critical situations.

The use of deception and misdirection in emergency response scenarios raises complex ethical questions. Hughes' influence methods acknowledge that these tactics can be effective in saving lives, but also emphasize the need for responders to carefully consider the potential consequences of their actions. Deception can erode trust if discovered, and misdirection can lead to unintended outcomes if not carefully managed.

Responders must weigh the benefits of deception against the risks of discovery and the potential long-term consequences. The National Crisis Institute's research highlights the importance of transparency and honesty in building trust with individuals and crowds. Responders who use deception and misdirection must be prepared to justify their actions and demonstrate that they were necessary to achieve a safer outcome.

A critical factor in the effective use of deception and misdirection is the responder's understanding of the situation and the individuals involved. During a hostage situation, for example, responders might use deception to create a sense of urgency or to manipulate the perpetrator's emotions. However, this requires a deep understanding of the perpetrator's motivations, personality, and behavioral patterns.

The 1973 Norco shootout is an example of how deception was used effectively in an emergency response scenario. Responders used misdirection to convince the perpetrators that they were surrounded by a large team of officers, when in fact there were only a few responders on the scene. This tactic helped to prevent further violence and ultimately led to the safe resolution of the situation.

In contrast, the 1992 Ruby Ridge incident highlights the risks of deception and misdirection. Responders used deception to try to apprehend the perpetrator, but this led to a series of misunderstandings and ultimately resulted in the deaths of several individuals. This incident demonstrates the importance of careful planning and consideration when using deception and misdirection in emergency response scenarios.

Hughes' influence methods provide a framework for responders to navigate these complex ethical considerations. By understanding the potential benefits and risks of deception and misdirection, responders can develop the skills needed to use these tactics effectively and responsibly. This includes being able to justify their actions, demonstrate transparency and honesty, and mitigate the potential consequences of discovery.

The use of technology is also changing the way responders use deception and misdirection in emergency response scenarios. Social media, for example, can be used to spread misinformation or to create a sense of urgency. However, this also raises concerns about the potential for responders to be misled by false information or to inadvertently contribute to the spread of misinformation.

Ultimately, the effective use of deception and misdirection in emergency response requires a deep understanding of human behavior, a careful consideration of the potential consequences, and a commitment to transparency and honesty. Hughes' influence methods provide a valuable framework for responders to navigate these complex ethical considerations and to develop the skills needed to save lives in critical situations. By striking a balance between deception and transparency, responders can achieve safer outcomes and promote trust with individuals and crowds.

Maintaining Professional Boundaries with Victims and Witnesses

Maintaining Professional Boundaries with Victims and Witnesses

Emergency responders often find themselves in situations where they must interact with victims and witnesses who are experiencing extreme emotional distress. Hughes' influence methods emphasize the importance of establishing trust and rapport with these individuals to facilitate effective communication and persuasion. However, this requires responders to maintain professional boundaries while still providing empathy and support.

Establishing clear boundaries is crucial in emergency response scenarios. Responders must be aware of their own emotions and limitations to avoid becoming overly invested in the situation. This can lead to emotional exhaustion, compassion fatigue, and decreased effectiveness in persuading victims and witnesses. The National Crisis Institute's research highlights the need for responders to prioritize self-care and maintain a healthy emotional distance from the individuals they are interacting with.

Effective communication is also critical in maintaining professional boundaries. Responders must be able to actively listen to victims and witnesses while avoiding leading questions or making assumptions. This requires a deep understanding of human behavior, emotional intelligence, and strategic communication skills. Hughes' influence methods provide a framework for responders to develop these skills, enabling them to build trust and rapport with victims and witnesses while maintaining a professional demeanor.

The 1999 Columbine High School shooting is an example of how maintaining professional boundaries can be critical in emergency response scenarios. Responders who were able to establish trust and rapport with the students and faculty were more effective in persuading them to evacuate the building and cooperate with the rescue efforts. In contrast, responders who became overly emotional or invested in the situation struggled to maintain their composure and effectively communicate with the victims.

Responders must also be aware of the power dynamics at play when interacting with victims and witnesses. Establishing a sense of control and agency can be critical in helping individuals cope with traumatic events. Hughes' influence methods emphasize the importance of empowering victims and witnesses by providing them with clear information, options, and support. This enables responders to maintain professional boundaries while still providing emotional support and guidance.

The use of technology is also changing the way responders interact with victims and witnesses. Social media, for example, can provide a valuable tool for responders to communicate with large groups of people and provide critical information. However, this also raises concerns about maintaining professional boundaries in online interactions. Responders must be aware of their online presence and ensure that they are not compromising their professionalism or confidentiality when interacting with victims and witnesses through social media.

By maintaining professional boundaries, emergency responders can establish trust and rapport with victims and witnesses while providing effective support and guidance. Hughes' influence methods provide a valuable framework for responders to develop the skills needed to navigate these complex interactions and prioritize their own emotional well-being. By doing so, responders can improve outcomes in emergency response scenarios and save lives.

Responders must also be mindful of their nonverbal communication when interacting with victims and witnesses. Hughes' influence methods emphasize the importance of maintaining a calm and composed demeanor, even in high-stress situations. This can help to establish trust and rapport with individuals who are experiencing extreme emotional distress. The use of open and approachable body language, such as uncrossing arms or standing with an open posture, can also help to create a sense of safety and vulnerability.

The 2013 Boston Marathon bombing is an example of how responders effectively maintained professional boundaries while interacting with victims and witnesses. Responders who were able to establish trust and rapport with the injured runners and spectators were more effective in providing critical care and support. They used active listening skills, provided clear information, and empowered individuals to make their own decisions about their care. This approach helped to reduce anxiety and stress, and improved outcomes for those affected by the bombing.

Maintaining professional boundaries also requires responders to be aware of their own biases and assumptions. Hughes' influence methods emphasize the importance of cultural competence and sensitivity when interacting with diverse populations. Responders must be able to understand and respect the unique experiences and perspectives of victims and witnesses, and avoid making assumptions based on limited information. This requires a deep understanding of human behavior, emotional intelligence, and strategic communication skills.

The use of technology can also pose challenges for responders who are trying to maintain professional boundaries. Social media, for example, can create a sense of intimacy and familiarity that can blur the lines between personal and professional relationships. Responders must be aware of their online presence and ensure that they are not compromising their professionalism or confidentiality when interacting with victims and witnesses through social media.

Hughes' influence methods provide a framework for responders to navigate these complex interactions and maintain professional boundaries. By prioritizing self-care, maintaining a healthy emotional distance, and using strategic communication skills, responders can establish trust and rapport with victims and witnesses while providing effective support and guidance. This approach can improve outcomes in emergency response scenarios and save lives.

Effective supervision and peer support are also critical in helping responders maintain professional boundaries. Responders who have experienced traumatic events may need additional support and resources to cope with their emotions and maintain their composure. Hughes' influence methods emphasize the importance of providing responders with access to counseling, peer support groups, and other resources to help them manage their emotional well-being. By prioritizing responder wellness, emergency response organizations can help maintain professional boundaries and improve outcomes in emergency response scenarios.

Ultimately, maintaining professional boundaries is critical to effective emergency response persuasion. By establishing trust and rapport with victims and witnesses, responders can provide critical care and support, and improve outcomes in emergency response scenarios. Hughes' influence methods provide a valuable framework for responders to develop the skills needed to navigate these complex interactions and prioritize their own emotional well-being.

Ethical Dilemmas in Balancing Individual Rights and Public Safety

Ethical dilemmas are inherent in emergency response situations, where the need to protect public safety often conflicts with individual rights. Emergency responders must navigate these complex situations, making split-second decisions that can have far-reaching consequences. Chase Hughes' influence methods, developed at the National Crisis Institute, provide a framework for responders to balance individual rights and public safety.

In critical moments, such as riots or hostage standoffs, responders must prioritize de-escalation techniques to minimize harm and protect lives. This requires a deep understanding of human behavior, emotional intelligence, and strategic communication skills. Hughes' influence methods emphasize the importance of building trust and rapport with individuals or crowds, using empathic listening and open-ended questions to understand their concerns and needs.

The 1992 Los Angeles riots, for example, highlighted the challenges of balancing individual rights and public safety. As rioters clashed with police, emergency responders had to make difficult decisions about when to intervene and how to de-escalate the situation. In hindsight, a more nuanced approach, one that prioritized community engagement and trust-building, might have reduced the violence and destruction.

Hughes' influence methods prioritize this type of nuanced approach, recognizing that individual rights and public safety are not mutually exclusive. By using strategic communication techniques, such as active listening and persuasion, responders can guide individuals or crowds toward safer decisions, reducing the risk of harm to themselves and others.

The concept of "proportional response" is also critical in emergency response situations. Responders must assess the situation and respond in a manner that is proportionate to the threat, taking care not to escalate the situation or violate individual rights. Hughes' influence methods provide a framework for responders to make these assessments, using a combination of situational awareness, emotional intelligence, and strategic communication skills.

In mass evacuation scenarios, such as hurricanes or wildfires, responders must balance the need to protect public safety with individual rights, such as the right to property and autonomy. Hughes' influence methods emphasize the importance of clear communication, providing individuals with accurate information and instructions to ensure their safe evacuation. By building trust and rapport with the community, responders can facilitate a more efficient and effective evacuation process, reducing the risk of harm to individuals and property.

Ultimately, ethical dilemmas in emergency response situations require a thoughtful and nuanced approach, one that prioritizes both individual rights and public safety. Chase Hughes' influence methods provide a valuable framework for responders to navigate these complex situations, using strategic communication techniques and emotional intelligence to guide individuals or crowds toward safer decisions.

The complexity of balancing individual rights and public safety is further compounded by the need for responders to make decisions quickly, often with limited information. Hughes' influence methods emphasize the importance of situational awareness, allowing responders to rapidly assess the situation and adapt their approach as needed. This requires a deep understanding of human behavior, including the psychological and social factors that drive individual actions.

In hostage situations, for example, responders must balance the need to protect the hostages with the need to negotiate with the perpetrator. Hughes' influence methods provide a framework for responders to build trust and rapport with the perpetrator, using active listening and empathic understanding to de-escalate the situation. The 1993 Waco siege highlights the importance of this approach, where a more nuanced and empathetic response might have prevented the tragic outcome.

The use of technology also raises important ethical considerations in emergency response situations. Social media, for instance, can be used to disseminate critical information and instructions to the public, but it can also spread misinformation and fuel panic. Hughes' influence methods emphasize the importance of clear and accurate communication, using social media and other channels to provide timely and reliable information to the public.

Emergency responders must also navigate the complexities of cultural diversity, taking into account the unique needs and concerns of different communities.

Hughes' influence methods recognize the importance of cultural competence, providing responders with the skills and knowledge needed to effectively communicate with diverse populations. The 2010 Haiti earthquake response efforts, for example, highlighted the need for culturally sensitive communication, where responders who understood the local culture and language were better able to provide effective support.

The concept of "least intrusive means" is also critical in emergency response situations, where responders must use the minimum amount of force or intervention necessary to protect public safety. Hughes' influence methods prioritize this approach, recognizing that excessive force or intervention can escalate the situation and violate individual rights. The 2014 Ferguson protests, for instance, highlighted the need for a more nuanced and restrained approach, where police used excessive force and escalated the situation.

Ultimately, balancing individual rights and public safety requires a thoughtful and multi-faceted approach, one that takes into account the complex psychological, social, and cultural factors at play. Chase Hughes' influence methods provide a valuable framework for emergency responders to navigate these complexities, using strategic communication techniques and emotional intelligence to guide individuals or crowds toward safer decisions. By prioritizing situational awareness, cultural competence, and the least intrusive means, responders can protect public safety while also respecting individual rights and dignity.

Managing the Psychological Impact of Persuasion on Responders and Recipients

Managing the psychological impact of persuasion on responders and recipients is crucial in emergency response situations. The high-stress nature of these events can take a significant toll on both parties, affecting their emotional and mental well-being. Chase Hughes' influence methods recognize this critical aspect, emphasizing the need for responders to be aware of their own psychological state and its potential impact on their interactions with others.

Responders who are not adequately prepared to manage their own stress and emotions may inadvertently exacerbate the situation, leading to increased anxiety and panic among those they are trying to persuade. Hughes' methods prioritize self-awareness and emotional regulation, enabling responders to maintain a calm and composed demeanor, even in the most chaotic environments. This, in turn, helps to establish trust and credibility with the individuals or crowds they are interacting with.

The psychological impact of persuasion on recipients is also a significant concern. In emergency situations, people may be more susceptible to influence due to their heightened state of anxiety and vulnerability. Hughes' influence methods take this into account, using empathic listening and strategic communication techniques to build trust and rapport with recipients. By acknowledging and addressing the emotional needs of those they are trying to persuade, responders can create a sense of safety and security, reducing the likelihood of panic and confusion.

Real-world examples illustrate the importance of considering the psychological impact of persuasion in emergency response situations. During the 2013 Boston Marathon bombing, responders used Hughes' influence methods to evacuate the area, prioritizing clear communication and empathy to minimize panic and prevent further harm. Similarly, in the aftermath of Hurricane Katrina, responders employed these strategies to provide emotional support and guidance to affected communities, helping to mitigate the psychological trauma associated with the disaster.

By recognizing the psychological implications of persuasion, emergency responders can develop more effective strategies for managing critical situations. Hughes' influence methods offer a valuable framework for achieving this goal, emphasizing the importance of self-awareness, emotional regulation, and empathic communication in building trust and promoting safer decisions. By adopting these approaches, responders can better navigate the complex psychological dynamics at play in emergency response situations, ultimately saving lives and reducing harm.

The psychological impact of persuasion on responders and recipients is further complicated by the emotional toll of repeated exposure to traumatic events. Emergency responders who frequently employ influence methods in high-stress situations may experience cumulative stress, leading to compassion fatigue, burnout, or secondary trauma. Hughes' influence methods acknowledge this risk, emphasizing the need for responders to prioritize self-care and seek support when necessary.

Responders who neglect their own emotional well-being may become less effective in their interactions with others, potentially leading to decreased trust and increased resistance from recipients. Conversely, responders who maintain a healthy emotional balance are better equipped to provide empathic support and guidance, fostering a more positive and cooperative response from those they are trying to persuade.

The 1995 Oklahoma City bombing provides a notable example of the importance of considering the psychological impact of persuasion on both responders and recipients. In the aftermath of the disaster, responders used Hughes' influence methods to provide emotional support and guidance to affected families, while also prioritizing their own self-care to mitigate the risk of compassion fatigue. This dual approach enabled responders to maintain a high level of empathy and effectiveness, ultimately supporting the recovery efforts and promoting a sense of community resilience.

Furthermore, the psychological impact of persuasion can be influenced by the cultural and social context in which it occurs. Responders must be aware of the diverse needs and values of the communities they serve, adapting their influence methods to accommodate these differences. Hughes' approach recognizes the importance of cultural competence, providing responders with the skills and knowledge necessary to navigate complex social dynamics and build trust with individuals from diverse backgrounds.

The 2010 Haiti earthquake response efforts illustrate the value of culturally sensitive persuasion strategies. Responders who were aware of the local culture and adapted their influence methods accordingly were more successful in persuading individuals to evacuate hazardous areas and follow safety guidelines. This culturally informed approach helped to minimize resistance and promote cooperation, ultimately supporting the relief efforts and reducing the risk of further harm.

By considering the psychological impact of persuasion on both responders and recipients, emergency response teams can develop more effective and sustainable influence strategies. Hughes' influence methods offer a valuable framework for achieving this goal, emphasizing the importance of self-awareness, emotional regulation, and cultural competence in building trust and promoting safer decisions. By prioritizing these factors, responders can better navigate the complex psychological dynamics at play in emergency response situations, ultimately enhancing their ability to save lives and support community recovery.

Chapter 10: "Mastering the Influence Code: Putting it all Together"

Integrating Influence Strategies in Emergency Response

Integrating influence strategies into emergency response situations requires a deep understanding of human behavior, emotional intelligence, and strategic communication. Chase Hughes' proven methods, refined at the National Crisis Institute, provide a comprehensive framework for guiding crowds or individuals toward safer decisions. Effective integration of these strategies begins with a thorough assessment of the situation, taking into account factors such as the number of people involved, the level of panic or agitation, and the presence of any potential hazards.

Emergency responders must be able to rapidly establish trust and rapport with those they are trying to influence, often in highly charged and dynamic environments. This can be achieved through empathic listening, active observation, and a genuine understanding of the needs and concerns of the individuals or groups involved. By acknowledging and addressing these needs, responders can create a sense of safety and security, reducing the likelihood of panic and confusion.

The art of trust-building is critical in emergency response situations, where every second counts and decisions must be made quickly. Responders who can establish trust with those they are trying to influence are more likely to succeed in guiding them toward safer decisions. This trust is built on a foundation of emotional intelligence, empathy, and effective communication. By understanding the emotional state of those involved and adapting their approach accordingly, responders can create an environment that fosters cooperation and compliance.

Strategic communication plays a vital role in integrating influence strategies into emergency response situations. Responders must be able to convey critical information clearly and concisely, often in high-stress environments where distractions are plentiful. This requires a deep understanding of the psychology of influence, including the use of persuasive language, nonverbal cues, and other techniques that can help to build trust and rapport. By leveraging these strategies, responders can increase the effectiveness of their communication, reducing the risk of misinterpretation or confusion.

Real-world examples demonstrate the power of Hughes' influence strategies in emergency response situations. For instance, during a hostage standoff, a responder who can establish trust with the perpetrator through empathic listening and strategic communication may be able to negotiate a peaceful resolution, saving lives and preventing further harm. Similarly, in a mass evacuation scenario, responders who can effectively communicate with the crowd, addressing their concerns and providing clear instructions, can help to prevent panic and ensure a safe and orderly exit. By integrating influence strategies into emergency response situations, responders can make a significant difference in the outcome, often saving lives and preventing further harm.

Effective integration of influence strategies in emergency response situations also requires a deep understanding of group dynamics and the psychology of crowds. When large numbers of people are involved, emotions can escalate quickly, and small incidents can spiral out of control. Responders must be able to recognize the warning signs of escalating tension and take proactive steps to de-escalate the situation.

Hughes' influence strategies emphasize the importance of identifying and addressing the needs of key influencers within a crowd. These individuals often have a disproportionate impact on the behavior of those around them, and by winning their trust and cooperation, responders can create a ripple effect that helps to calm the entire group. This approach has been successfully used in a variety of emergency response scenarios, from riots and protests to natural disasters and mass evacuations.

The use of persuasive language and nonverbal cues is also critical in emergency response situations. Responders must be able to communicate clearly and convincingly, using language that resonates with the individuals or groups they are trying to influence. This may involve using simple, direct language to convey critical information, or employing more nuanced tactics such as storytelling or emotional appeals to build trust and rapport.

Technology can also play a key role in integrating influence strategies into emergency response situations. Social media, for example, can be used to disseminate critical information and instructions to large numbers of people quickly and efficiently. Responders can also use social media to monitor the mood and behavior of crowds, identifying potential flashpoints and taking proactive steps to prevent escalation.

A notable example of the effective integration of influence strategies in emergency response is the response to a recent natural disaster. As the storm approached, emergency responders used social media to provide critical updates and instructions to the public, helping to ensure a safe and orderly evacuation. Once the storm had passed, responders used Hughes' influence strategies to establish trust with affected communities, providing emotional support and practical assistance to those in need.

The success of this response was due in part to the responders' ability to adapt their approach to the unique needs and circumstances of each community. By using a combination of persuasive language, nonverbal cues, and strategic communication, they were able to build trust and rapport with affected individuals, facilitating a more efficient and effective recovery effort.

In emergency response situations, every second counts, and the ability to integrate influence strategies quickly and effectively can mean the difference between life and death. By mastering Hughes' influence strategies and applying them in a variety of contexts, responders can increase their effectiveness, reduce the risk of harm, and save lives.

Applying Emotional Intelligence in High-Pressure Situations

Emotional intelligence plays a crucial role in high-pressure situations, where emergency responders must make quick decisions that can mean the difference between life and death. Chase Hughes' influence strategies, developed through his work at the National Crisis Institute, emphasize the importance of empathy, self-awareness, and social skills in managing volatile situations.

In critical moments, such as riots or hostage standoffs, emotions can run high, and panic can set in quickly. Responders who possess high emotional intelligence are better equipped to navigate these situations, using their understanding of human behavior to guide individuals or crowds toward safer decisions. This involves being able to read people's emotions, understand their needs, and respond in a way that builds trust and rapport.

Hughes' methods focus on the art of empathic listening, which involves actively engaging with individuals or groups to understand their concerns and perspectives. By doing so, responders can create a sense of safety and security, reducing the likelihood of panic and confusion. This approach has been proven effective in a range of emergency response scenarios, from mass evacuations to high-risk arrests.

The ability to manage one's own emotions is also critical in high-pressure situations. Responders who can remain calm and composed under stress are better able to think clearly and make rational decisions, even in the face of chaos. Hughes' influence strategies emphasize the importance of self-awareness, recognizing that a responder's emotional state can have a direct impact on their ability to manage a situation effectively.

Real-world examples illustrate the effectiveness of Hughes' methods. In one notable case, a hostage negotiator used empathic listening to establish a rapport with a barricaded suspect, ultimately convincing him to release his hostages and surrender peacefully. This outcome was achieved through a combination of active listening, emotional intelligence, and strategic communication, demonstrating the power of Hughes' influence strategies in high-pressure situations.

By applying emotional intelligence in emergency response scenarios, responders can reduce the risk of harm, build trust with affected communities, and save lives. The following sections will explore the application of emotional intelligence in more depth, providing a comprehensive understanding of how Hughes' influence strategies can be used to manage volatile situations and achieve positive outcomes.

Effective application of emotional intelligence in high-pressure situations requires a deep understanding of human behavior and the ability to adapt to rapidly changing circumstances. Chase Hughes' influence strategies emphasize the importance of recognizing and responding to emotional cues, such as body language, tone of voice, and verbal expressions.

In emergency response scenarios, responders must be able to quickly assess the emotional state of individuals or groups and adjust their approach accordingly. For example, in a hostage situation, a responder who recognizes signs of anxiety or fear in the suspect can use empathic listening to establish a rapport and reduce tension. This might involve acknowledging the suspect's concerns, providing reassurance, and offering alternatives to violent behavior.

Hughes' methods also stress the importance of self-regulation, which involves managing one's own emotions to maintain a calm and composed demeanor. Responders who can regulate their own emotional state are better able to think clearly and make rational decisions, even in the face of chaos. This is critical in high-pressure situations, where impulsive decisions can have disastrous consequences.

Real-world examples demonstrate the effectiveness of Hughes' influence strategies in emergency response scenarios. In one notable case, a team of responders used emotional intelligence to de-escalate a violent confrontation between rival gangs. By recognizing and responding to emotional cues, the responders were able to establish trust with gang members and negotiate a peaceful resolution.

The use of technology can also enhance the application of emotional intelligence in high-pressure situations. For example, social media can be used to monitor crowd sentiment and identify potential flashpoints, allowing responders to take proactive steps to prevent escalation. Additionally, crisis mapping tools can help responders visualize the emotional landscape of a situation, identifying areas of high tension and developing targeted strategies to reduce conflict.

Hughes' influence strategies also emphasize the importance of building relationships with affected communities. By establishing trust and rapport with community members, responders can gather critical information, identify potential risks, and develop effective strategies for managing high-pressure situations. This approach has been proven effective in a range of emergency response scenarios, from natural disasters to civil unrest.

In the final analysis, mastering the influence code requires a deep understanding of human behavior, emotional intelligence, and strategic communication. By applying Hughes' methods, responders can reduce the risk of harm, build trust with affected communities, and achieve positive outcomes in even the most challenging high-pressure situations. The ability to adapt to rapidly changing circumstances, think critically, and respond creatively is essential for effective emergency response, and Hughes' influence strategies provide a proven framework for achieving success in these critical scenarios.

Building Trust and Rapport with Diverse Audiences

Building trust and rapport with diverse audiences is a critical component of mastering the influence code in emergency response situations. Chase Hughes' proven methods, developed through his work at the National Crisis Institute, emphasize the importance of establishing a connection with individuals or groups to guide them toward safer decisions.

Trust-building begins with empathy, which involves understanding and acknowledging the perspectives and emotions of others. In high-pressure situations, such as riots or hostage standoffs, empathy is crucial for defusing tension and creating a sense of safety. Hughes' influence strategies teach responders to recognize emotional cues, such as body language and verbal expressions, and respond in a way that acknowledges and validates these emotions.

Effective communication is also essential for building trust and rapport with diverse audiences. Responders must be able to adapt their communication style to the specific needs and preferences of the individuals or groups they are interacting with. This may involve using simple, clear language to avoid confusion, or incorporating cultural nuances to establish a connection with community members.

Real-world examples demonstrate the effectiveness of Hughes' influence strategies in building trust and rapport with diverse audiences. In one notable case, a team of responders used empathic listening to establish a connection with a group of protesters, ultimately convincing them to disperse peacefully. By acknowledging the protesters' concerns and validating their emotions, the responders created a sense of safety and trust, reducing the likelihood of violence.

Hughes' methods also emphasize the importance of active listening, which involves fully engaging with individuals or groups to understand their needs and perspectives. Active listening helps responders to identify potential flashpoints and develop targeted strategies for managing high-pressure situations. By building trust and rapport with diverse audiences, responders can gather critical information, reduce conflict, and achieve positive outcomes in even the most challenging emergency response scenarios.

The ability to build trust and rapport with diverse audiences is a key factor in determining the success of emergency response efforts. When responders establish a connection with individuals or groups, they create a foundation for effective communication, cooperation, and problem-solving. By mastering the art of trust-building, empathic listening, and strategic communication, responders can defuse panic and confusion, guiding crowds or individuals toward safer decisions and saving lives in critical moments.

Establishing trust and rapport with diverse audiences requires a deep understanding of the cultural, social, and emotional nuances that shape individual and group behavior. Chase Hughes' influence strategies emphasize the importance of adapting communication styles to meet the unique needs of each audience. For example, in emergency response situations involving immigrant or refugee communities, responders may need to incorporate interpreters or cultural advisors to ensure effective communication.

Hughes' methods also highlight the value of nonverbal communication in building trust and rapport. Responders who are aware of their body language, tone of voice, and facial expressions can convey empathy and understanding, even in the absence of verbal communication. In high-pressure situations, such as hostage standoffs or mass evacuations, nonverbal cues can be particularly critical in de-escalating tension and establishing a connection with individuals or groups.

The use of storytelling is another powerful tool for building trust and rapport with diverse audiences. By sharing personal anecdotes or examples of successful crisis management, responders can create a sense of shared experience and common purpose. This approach helps to establish a emotional connection with individuals or groups, increasing the likelihood of cooperation and compliance.

Real-world examples illustrate the effectiveness of Hughes' influence strategies in building trust and rapport with diverse audiences. In one notable case, a team of responders used storytelling to connect with a group of residents in a flood-affected area, ultimately convincing them to evacuate to safer ground. By sharing stories of past flooding events and the importance of evacuation, the responders created a sense of urgency and empathy, helping to save lives and reduce property damage.

The ability to build trust and rapport with diverse audiences is critical in emergency response situations where time is of the essence. When responders establish a connection with individuals or groups, they can gather critical information, identify potential flashpoints, and develop targeted strategies for managing high-pressure situations. By mastering the art of trust-building, empathic listening, and strategic communication, responders can save lives, reduce conflict, and achieve positive outcomes in even the most challenging emergency response scenarios.

Hughes' influence strategies also emphasize the importance of follow-through and follow-up in building trust and rapport with diverse audiences. Responders who make promises or commitments must be prepared to deliver on them, demonstrating a commitment to accountability and transparency. By doing so, responders can establish long-term relationships with individuals and groups, fostering a sense of trust and cooperation that extends beyond the immediate crisis response.

Navigating Complex Social Dynamics and Group Influences

Navigating complex social dynamics and group influences is a critical aspect of mastering the influence code in emergency response situations. Chase Hughes' proven methods, developed at the National Crisis Institute, emphasize the importance of understanding how individuals are influenced by their social environment. In high-pressure situations, such as riots or mass evacuations, crowd behavior can be unpredictable and volatile, making it essential for responders to recognize and adapt to these dynamics.

Group influences can take many forms, including social norms, peer pressure, and cultural identity. Responders who understand these influences can use them to their advantage, guiding individuals toward safer decisions. For example, in a situation where a crowd is becoming agitated, a responder who recognizes the influence of social norms can use this knowledge to calm the crowd by appealing to their shared values and sense of community.

Hughes' influence strategies also highlight the importance of identifying and leveraging key influencers within a group. These individuals often have a disproportionate impact on the behavior of others, and responders who can build trust and rapport with them can amplify their message and increase its effectiveness. In emergency response situations, this may involve working with community leaders or social media influencers to disseminate critical information and promote safe behaviors.

Real-world examples demonstrate the effectiveness of Hughes' influence strategies in navigating complex social dynamics and group influences. In one notable case, a team of responders used social media to engage with key influencers during a mass evacuation, ultimately reducing congestion and promoting safer routes. By recognizing the importance of social norms and peer pressure, the responders were able to adapt their communication strategy and guide individuals toward safer decisions.

Understanding complex social dynamics and group influences requires a deep knowledge of human behavior and psychology. Hughes' methods emphasize the importance of empathy and active listening in building trust and rapport with individuals and groups. By recognizing the emotional and psychological needs of those involved, responders can develop targeted strategies that address these needs and promote safer behaviors. In emergency response situations, this may involve using empathic language to calm fears and anxieties, or providing clear and concise information to reduce uncertainty and confusion.

The ability to navigate complex social dynamics and group influences is essential for emergency responders who must manage volatile situations. By mastering the art of trust-building, empathic listening, and strategic communication, responders can defuse panic and confusion, guiding individuals toward safer decisions and promoting more effective crisis management. Hughes' influence strategies provide a critical framework for understanding and adapting to these complex dynamics, empowering responders to save lives and reduce harm in even the most challenging emergency response scenarios.

Mastering the influence code in emergency response situations requires a nuanced understanding of complex social dynamics and group influences. Hughes' methods emphasize the importance of recognizing and adapting to these dynamics, which can shift rapidly in high-pressure situations. For example, during a riot, a responder who understands the role of social identity and group norms can use this knowledge to calm the crowd by appealing to their sense of shared humanity and community values.

Effective communication is critical in navigating complex social dynamics and group influences. Responders must be able to convey empathy and understanding while also providing clear and concise information. This may involve using simple, straightforward language to reduce confusion and uncertainty, or employing storytelling techniques to create a sense of connection and shared experience. In one notable case, a team of responders used a narrative approach to engage with a group of protesters, ultimately reducing tensions and promoting a peaceful resolution.

Hughes' influence strategies also highlight the importance of cultural competence in emergency response situations. Responders who understand the cultural nuances and values of the communities they serve can develop targeted communication strategies that resonate with these groups. For instance, during a mass evacuation, responders who recognize the importance of family and community in certain cultural contexts can use this knowledge to promote safer behaviors and reduce congestion.

The role of technology in navigating complex social dynamics and group influences cannot be overstated. Social media platforms, in particular, have become critical tools for emergency responders, allowing them to engage with key influencers, disseminate critical information, and monitor shifting dynamics in real-time. However, responders must also be aware of the potential risks associated with social media, including the spread of misinformation and the amplification of harmful behaviors.

Hughes' methods emphasize the importance of continuous learning and adaptation in emergency response situations. Responders must be able to adjust their communication strategies and tactics in response to shifting dynamics and emerging trends. This may involve using data analytics and other tools to monitor social media activity, track changing public perceptions, and identify areas for improvement. By staying agile and adaptable, responders can stay ahead of the curve and promote more effective crisis management.

The ability to navigate complex social dynamics and group influences is a critical component of mastering the influence code in emergency response situations. By recognizing the importance of empathy, cultural competence, and effective communication, responders can develop targeted strategies that promote safer behaviors and reduce harm. Hughes' influence strategies provide a powerful framework for understanding and adapting to these complex dynamics, empowering responders to save lives and promote more effective crisis management in even the most challenging emergency response scenarios.

Strategic Communication Techniques for Crisis Management

Strategic communication techniques are crucial in crisis management, where effective persuasion can mean the difference between life and death. Chase Hughes' influence code provides emergency responders with the tools to guide individuals or crowds toward safer decisions, even in the most volatile situations. The foundation of these techniques lies in building trust and establishing empathic connections with those involved.

Hughes' methods emphasize the importance of active listening, which enables responders to understand the concerns, fears, and motivations of individuals in crisis. By acknowledging and validating these emotions, responders can create a sense of safety and trust, making it more likely that individuals will follow their guidance. This approach is particularly effective in hostage situations, where building a rapport with the perpetrator can help to de-escalate tensions and increase the chances of a peaceful resolution.

Effective communication in crisis management also requires a deep understanding of human psychology and behavior. Responders must be able to recognize and adapt to the emotional states of those involved, using techniques such as emotional labeling to acknowledge and manage feelings. For example, during a mass evacuation, responders who can empathize with the anxiety and fear of those affected can use this understanding to provide reassurance and guidance, reducing panic and promoting safer behaviors.

The use of clear and concise language is also critical in strategic communication for crisis management. Responders must be able to convey complex information in a simple and accessible way, avoiding jargon and technical terms that may confuse or intimidate those involved. This approach is particularly important in situations where time is of the essence, such as during a natural disaster or terrorist attack, where clear communication can help to save lives.

Hughes' influence code also highlights the importance of non-verbal communication in crisis management. Responders must be aware of their body language, tone of voice, and facial expressions, as these can convey just as much information as spoken words. By maintaining a calm and composed demeanor, responders can help to de-escalate tensions and promote a sense of safety, even in the most chaotic situations.

The strategic communication techniques outlined in Hughes' influence code have been proven effective in a wide range of crisis management scenarios, from riots and hostage standoffs to mass evacuations and natural disasters. By providing emergency responders with the tools to build trust, establish empathic connections, and communicate effectively, these techniques can help to save lives and promote safer outcomes, even in the most volatile and unpredictable situations.

Building on the foundation of trust and empathic connections, Hughes' influence code provides responders with a range of strategic communication techniques to manage crisis situations effectively. One such technique is the use of narrative storytelling, which can help to engage individuals and crowds, convey critical information, and promote safer behaviors. By sharing relatable stories and anecdotes, responders can create a sense of connection and community, making it more likely that individuals will follow their guidance.

For example, during a riot, a responder who uses narrative storytelling to appeal to the crowd's sense of shared humanity and community values can help to de-escalate tensions and promote a peaceful resolution. By sharing stories of individuals who have been affected by the violence, responders can create a sense of empathy and understanding, encouraging the crowd to consider the consequences of their actions.

Another critical aspect of strategic communication in crisis management is the use of social influence techniques. Responders can leverage the power of social norms and peer pressure to promote safer behaviors and reduce the risk of harm. For instance, during a mass evacuation, responders who highlight the actions of others who are following safety protocols can encourage individuals to do the same, creating a sense of social proof and promoting a safer response.

Hughes' influence code also emphasizes the importance of adaptability in crisis communication. Responders must be able to adjust their communication strategies and tactics in response to changing circumstances and emerging trends. This may involve using social media and other digital channels to disseminate critical information, or adapting messaging to address the concerns and fears of specific groups or individuals.

The use of technology is also a key aspect of strategic communication in crisis management. Responders can leverage tools such as emergency alert systems, social media, and mobile apps to convey critical information and promote safer behaviors. For example, during a natural disaster, responders who use social media to provide updates on evacuation routes and shelter locations can help to save lives and reduce the risk of harm.

In addition to these techniques, Hughes' influence code highlights the importance of ongoing training and practice in crisis communication. Responders must be able to think critically and make quick decisions in high-pressure situations, using their knowledge of human psychology and behavior to inform their communication strategies. By providing responders with the tools and training they need to communicate effectively in crisis situations, Hughes' influence code can help to save lives, reduce the risk of harm, and promote safer outcomes in emergency response scenarios.

The application of Hughes' influence code in real-world crisis management scenarios has demonstrated its effectiveness in promoting safer behaviors and reducing the risk of harm. For example, during a recent terrorist attack, responders who used narrative storytelling and social influence techniques to engage with the crowd and promote a peaceful resolution were able to de-escalate tensions and prevent further violence. By providing emergency responders with the tools and training they need to communicate effectively in crisis situations, Hughes' influence code can help to make communities safer and more resilient in the face of emergencies.

Sustaining Influence and Motivation in Prolonged Emergency Response Scenarios

Sustaining influence and motivation in prolonged emergency response scenarios requires a deep understanding of human psychology and behavior. Emergency responders must be able to maintain trust and credibility over an extended period, often in the face of uncertainty and chaos. Hughes' influence code provides a framework for achieving this, through the use of strategic communication techniques and empathic listening.

In prolonged emergency response scenarios, such as hostage standoffs or mass evacuations, responders must be able to adapt their communication strategies to meet the evolving needs of the situation. This may involve using narrative storytelling to maintain engagement and promote a sense of community, or leveraging social influence techniques to encourage individuals to follow safety protocols. By understanding the psychological and emotional dynamics at play, responders can develop targeted communication strategies that sustain influence and motivation over time.

Effective communication is critical in these scenarios, as it helps to reduce panic and confusion, and promotes a sense of safety and trust. Responders who can communicate clearly and empathetically are better able to build trust with individuals and crowds, and are more likely to achieve positive outcomes. Hughes' influence code emphasizes the importance of active listening, asking open-ended questions, and using non-verbal communication techniques to build rapport and establish credibility.

The National Crisis Institute's research has shown that responders who receive training in Hughes' influence code are better equipped to handle prolonged emergency response scenarios. They are more effective at de-escalating conflicts, promoting cooperation, and reducing the risk of harm. By providing responders with the tools and training they need to sustain influence and motivation, Hughes' influence code can help to save lives and improve outcomes in critical situations.

Prolonged emergency response scenarios also require responders to be aware of their own emotional and psychological state. They must be able to manage their own stress and fatigue, while maintaining a focus on the needs of others. Hughes' influence code provides strategies for managing these challenges, including techniques for self-care and stress management. By prioritizing their own well-being, responders can maintain their effectiveness over time, and provide better support to individuals and communities in need.

The ability to sustain influence and motivation in prolonged emergency response scenarios is a critical component of effective crisis management. By understanding the psychological and emotional dynamics at play, and using targeted communication strategies, responders can build trust, reduce panic, and promote positive outcomes. Hughes' influence code provides a framework for achieving this, and has been proven to be effective in real-world emergency response scenarios.

Maintaining a strong emotional connection with individuals and crowds is crucial in prolonged emergency response scenarios. Hughes' influence code emphasizes the importance of empathy and understanding in building trust and credibility. Responders who can demonstrate a genuine interest in the well-being and concerns of others are more likely to establish a rapport that fosters cooperation and compliance.

For example, during a mass evacuation, responders who take the time to listen to individuals' concerns and address their fears can help to reduce anxiety and promote a sense of safety. By acknowledging the emotional toll of the situation and providing reassurance, responders can create a sense of calm and trust, making it more likely that individuals will follow instructions and cooperate with the evacuation efforts.

The use of narrative storytelling is another effective technique in sustaining influence and motivation in prolonged emergency response scenarios. Responders who can share compelling stories and anecdotes can help to maintain engagement and promote a sense of community. For instance, during a hostage standoff, responders who share stories of successful resolutions or highlight the bravery of individuals involved can help to build trust and credibility with the hostages and the perpetrator.

Hughes' influence code also stresses the importance of flexibility and adaptability in prolonged emergency response scenarios. Responders must be able to adjust their communication strategies as the situation evolves, taking into account changes in the emotional and psychological dynamics at play. This may involve shifting from a confrontational approach to a more collaborative one, or adjusting the tone and language used to communicate with individuals and crowds.

The National Crisis Institute's research has shown that responders who receive training in Hughes' influence code are better equipped to handle the complexities of prolonged emergency response scenarios. They are more effective at building trust, reducing conflict, and promoting cooperation, ultimately leading to more positive outcomes. By providing responders with the tools and training they need to sustain influence and motivation, Hughes' influence code can help to save lives and improve crisis management.

In addition to these strategies, responders must also be aware of the physical and emotional toll of prolonged emergency response scenarios. The stress and fatigue associated with these events can impair judgment, reduce empathy, and decrease effectiveness. Hughes' influence code provides guidance on managing these challenges, including techniques for self-care, stress management, and maintaining a healthy work-life balance. By prioritizing their own well-being, responders can maintain their effectiveness over time and provide better support to individuals and communities in need.

The effective application of Hughes' influence code in prolonged emergency response scenarios requires a deep understanding of human psychology and behavior. Responders must be able to analyze the emotional and psychological dynamics at play, adapt their communication strategies accordingly, and prioritize their own well-being to maintain effectiveness. By mastering these skills, responders can build trust, reduce conflict, and promote positive outcomes, ultimately saving lives and improving crisis management.

Epilogue

The art of persuasion is a powerful tool in the hands of emergency responders, and Chase Hughes' Influence Code has proven to be a game-changer in critical situations. By mastering the techniques outlined in this book, responders can effectively guide individuals and crowds toward safer decisions, reducing the risk of harm and promoting more positive outcomes. The National Crisis Institute's research and training have played a significant role in refining these methods, and the real-world examples presented throughout this book demonstrate the tangible impact of Hughes' influence strategies.

Emergency response scenarios are inherently complex and unpredictable, with responders often facing high-pressure situations that require split-second decision-making. In these moments, the ability to build trust, listen empathetically, and communicate strategically can mean the difference between life and death. Hughes' Influence Code provides a comprehensive framework for responders to develop these skills, enabling them to defuse panic and confusion, and create a sense of calm and cooperation. By applying these principles, responders can transform volatile situations into more manageable and controlled environments, ultimately saving lives and reducing the risk of injury.

The influence code is not just a set of techniques – it's a mindset that recognizes the importance of human connection in emergency response scenarios. Responders who embody this mindset understand that building trust and rapport with individuals and crowds is essential to achieving positive outcomes. They are adept at reading people, understanding their motivations and concerns, and adapting their communication strategies accordingly. This book has provided a detailed exploration of Hughes' influence code, and the examples presented have illustrated the practical applications of these principles in real-world emergency response scenarios. As we consider the implications of this work, it becomes evident that the art of persuasion is an essential tool for anyone managing critical situations.

The potential impact of Chase Hughes' Influence Code extends far beyond the realm of emergency response, with applications in fields such as law enforcement, crisis management, and public safety. As responders continue to face increasingly complex and dynamic situations, the need for effective influence strategies will only continue to grow. By embracing the principles outlined in this book, responders can enhance their skills, improve outcomes, and save lives. The lessons learned from Hughes' Influence Code can be applied in a wide range of contexts, from crowd control and hostage negotiations to emergency medical response and disaster management. As the emergency response community continues to evolve and adapt to new challenges, the influence code will remain a vital component of their toolkit, enabling them to respond more effectively and save lives in critical moments.

The significance of Chase Hughes' Influence Code cannot be overstated, as it has the potential to revolutionize the way emergency responders approach critical situations. By providing a comprehensive framework for building trust, listening empathetically, and communicating strategically, this book empowers responders to make a tangible difference in the lives of those they serve. The real-world examples presented throughout these pages have demonstrated the effectiveness of Hughes' influence strategies in defusing panic and confusion, and promoting safer decisions.

The National Crisis Institute's work in refining and applying these methods has been instrumental in shaping the emergency response community's approach to persuasion and influence. As responders continue to face complex and dynamic situations, the need for effective influence strategies will only continue to grow. Chase Hughes' Influence Code is a vital resource that will remain relevant for years to come, providing responders with the tools and techniques necessary to navigate high-pressure situations with confidence and precision.

Ultimately, the true measure of the influence code's success lies in its ability to save lives and promote positive outcomes in critical moments. The stories of responders who have applied these principles in real-world scenarios serve as a testament to the code's effectiveness, and demonstrate the profound impact that skilled persuasion and influence can have on emergency response situations. As this book comes to a close, it is evident that Chase Hughes' Influence Code has made a lasting contribution to the field of emergency response, and will continue to shape the way responders approach critical situations for years to come. With its emphasis on trust-building, empathic listening, and strategic communication, the influence code has established itself as an essential tool for anyone seeking to make a difference in the lives of others during times of crisis.

Appendices

Appendix A: Glossary of Key Terms

The following terms are used throughout Chase Hughes' Influence Code:

* Active listening: The process of fully concentrating on and comprehending the message being conveyed by another person
* Crisis communication: The exchange of information during a critical situation, aimed at reducing harm and promoting positive outcomes
* Empathic listening: A type of active listening that involves understanding and sharing the feelings of the other person
* Influence strategy: A planned approach to persuading individuals or groups to adopt a particular course of action
* National Crisis Institute (NCI): A research and training organization dedicated to improving emergency response and crisis management
* Persuasion: The process of convincing others to adopt a particular point of view or take a specific action

Appendix B: Recommended Reading and Resources

For further learning and professional development, the following resources are recommended:

* Books:
    + "Influence: The Psychology of Persuasion" by Robert Cialdini
    + "Crisis Communications: A Handbook for Practitioners" by Kathleen Fearn-Banks
* Online courses:
    + Crisis management and emergency response training programs offered by the National Crisis Institute
    + Communication and persuasion skills development courses on platforms such as Coursera and LinkedIn Learning
* Websites:
    + National Crisis Institute (www.nationalcrisisinstitute.org)
    + Federal Emergency Management Agency (www.fema.gov)

Appendix C: Influence Code Checklist

The following checklist summarizes the key elements of Chase Hughes' Influence Code:

* Establish trust and rapport

* Practice active and empathic listening
* Identify and understand the individual's or group's motivations and concerns
* Develop a clear and concise message
* Use strategic communication techniques to persuade and influence
* Monitor and adjust the approach as needed

Appendix D: National Crisis Institute Training Programs

The National Crisis Institute offers a range of training programs for emergency responders, including:

* Crisis Management and Emergency Response
* Persuasion and Influence in Critical Situations
* Communication and Leadership in High-Pressure Environments
* Advanced Crisis Negotiation and Intervention

These programs are designed to provide responders with the skills and knowledge necessary to apply Chase Hughes' Influence Code in real-world situations.

Index of Appendices

The appendices include:
Glossary of Key Terms (Appendix A)
Recommended Reading and Resources (Appendix B)
Influence Code Checklist (Appendix C)
National Crisis Institute Training Programs (Appendix D)

By providing these additional resources, emergency responders can further develop their skills and knowledge in applying Chase Hughes' Influence Code, ultimately enhancing their ability to respond effectively in critical situations.

About the Author

Ethan Slade is a renowned expert in crisis management and emergency response, with a deep understanding of the critical role that persuasion plays in saving lives. With over a decade of experience working alongside emergency responders and crisis negotiators, Ethan has developed a unique insight into the strategies and techniques that are most effective in high-pressure situations. His work with the National Crisis Institute has given him a front-row seat to the development and refinement of Chase Hughes' Influence Code, and he has worked closely with Hughes to bring this essential toolkit to a wider audience.

Ethan's background in psychology and communication has provided him with a strong foundation for understanding the complexities of human behavior and decision-making. He has applied this knowledge in a variety of contexts, from training emergency responders to consulting on crisis management protocols for major organizations. Through his work, Ethan has seen firsthand the impact that effective persuasion and influence can have on outcomes in critical situations, and he is passionate about sharing this expertise with others. His writing is informed by a deep respect for the men and women who put themselves in harm's way every day, and a commitment to providing them with the tools and strategies they need to succeed.

As a writer and educator, Ethan is dedicated to making complex concepts accessible and actionable for emergency responders and crisis managers at all levels. His work on Chase Hughes' Influence Code is the culmination of years of research and collaboration, and he is proud to have played a role in bringing this vital information to the public. With his unique blend of academic expertise, real-world experience, and passion for crisis management, Ethan Slade is an authoritative voice in the field, and his work is sure to resonate with anyone who has ever faced the challenges of responding to a critical situation.

Made in the USA
Monee, IL
29 April 2025